Other books by D

The Day They Padlocked The Church

The ACLU and America's Freedoms

Homosexual Politics: Road To Ruin For America

New Age Globalism

**Humanist Agenda for Building
A New World without God**

About The Author

H. Edward Rowe is president of *Christian Mandate for America*, a ministry which Dr. D. James Kennedy of Coral Ridge Presbyterian Church serves as Chairman. The purpose of *Christian Mandate* is to mobilize Christians nationally in obedience to the biblical principles which are foundational to good government.

Formerly Dr. Rowe served as President of the Church League of America, as Executive Director of *Coral Ridge Ministries*, Dr. D. James Kennedy's television organization in Fort Lauderdale, and earlier as Executive Director of *The Religious Roundtable*.

Dr. Rowe's past experience includes a decade of service as President of the *Christian Freedom Foundation* and Editor of its publication, *Christian Economics*.

Dr. Ed Rowe is author of a book titled *Save America: The Power of the Christian Citizen* (Revell, 1976). His second book, *The Day They Padlocked the Church* (Huntington House, 1983), is an eyewitness account of the Nebraska religious liberty crisis of September and October, 1982, and a clear warning of the rising tide of state tyranny in America.

More recent smaller books by Ed Rowe bear the titles *Homosexual Politics—Road To Ruin For America* and *The ACLU and America's Freedoms*.

H. Edward Rowe holds the Bachelor of Arts degree from Gordon College, The Master of Theology degree from Dallas Theological Seminary, and the Doctor of Divinity degree from the California Graduate School of Theology.

Ed has written hundreds of editorials, articles, pamphlets and radio scripts, has conducted broadcasts on a wide range of subjects relevant to the application of Christianity within all spheres of life, and has preached and lectured widely on freedom themes and vital issues of today.

New Age Globalism

Humanist Agenda for Building
A New World without God

Dr. H. Edward Rowe

GROWTH PUBLISHING
P.O. Box 661 • Herndon, Virginia 22070
1 (800) 426-8095
In Virginia (703) 450-6460 or
1 (800) 533-4037

Dedication

To my children—David, Becky, Ruth and Debbie, in the hope that they and their children will never be compelled to live under the nightmare of globalist tyranny described in this book.

Foreword

A substitute school teacher told me recently that he tried to start a Junior High class period by reciting the pledge of allegiance, only to find that 16 of the 30 students did not know it!

At a law school graduation ceremony, 60 graduates refused to stand during the playing of the national anthem. One high school discontinued the practice of playing the anthem each morning because the students were so disrespectful.

Last year the largest number of college students in the history of America refused to register for the draft. And polls show a growing disenchantment with free enterprise, democracy, and the American way of life. In fact, this disenchantment tends to increase in direct proportion to a student's time spent in the classroom.

From all over the nation letters are received regularly by the President of the United States lecturing him on his "belligerent attitude toward the Russians." Students who can barely write, spell, or compose a complete sentence advise our President that the greatest danger in the world is nuclear armament. Students who cannot spell "nuclear" advise him to seek peace with the Russians at any cost.

The advice from students in a Miami school system —where 48 percent did not know the location of Chicago, Washington, or the capital of their state—was that "the freedom loving leaders of Russia want peace with America."

Even the former governor of one of our states, a victim of five years of graduate school studies said, "We must assume that the Russian leaders are honorable men"—just one week before they shot the Korean airliner out of the sky, murdering 269 people, including the most anti-Communist Congressman in the country, Dr. Larry McDonald.

I will never forget the shock a group of parents registered when I showed them that their children's sixth grade social studies textbook said that "after World War II the people of Russia helped the Polish people establish Communism as their form of government." They said nothing about how they betrayed their former allies and at the point of tanks and guns forced a Communist puppet government on that freedom-loving nation.

Where do all these weird notions come from? Is this what parents are teaching their children at home? Do Sunday School teachers give this instruction to our young? Not hardly! What do these students all have in common? They attend government controlled schools (popularly known as the public schools).

The humanist "educrats" who control our government schools from the teachers' colleges to the curriculum are not there to raise up a new generation of American patriots who would defend their freedoms to the death. To them that is "passé." They are trying to raise up a new world order of "internationalists" or "one worlders." They are convinced that nationalism is the cause of wars, poverty, disease, and ignorance. They teach that only by raising up a generation of young people who see beyond the borders of their nation to a world order of peace and brotherhood among all nations will we solve these problems. They are convinced that world socialism will rid the world of greed and all will have enough.

This all sounds plausible in the idealistic environment of the classroom. The problem is, socialism has never worked to upgrade the standard of life in any country where it has been tried; yet these new age teachers would bring it to America. Socialism has been more accurately called "shared poverty," for that is what it has done for every country that has adopted it.

Who are these people that would turn the greatest system of government in the world and the best economy for the largest number of people into a pawn in the hands of an international elite who make all the decisions for "little brother"? That is what this book is all about, the who, why, and what of global education. It is the "wave of the future" in government-controlled education as long as secular humanists continue to determine course curriculum.

You owe it to yourself, your children, and our

present generation of classroom students to inform
yourself on this subject. For only an informed citizenry
will be able to awaken enough people to expel this
philosophy from our schools and our media before it
becomes so entrenched that it reduces our commitment
to individual freedom and the preservation of our re-
public.

You're going to hear a lot about "globalism" during
the next few years, either because it has been imposed
upon us by the humanists who would be our masters
or because you have taken steps to inform your circle
of influence to the extent that Americans can vote in-
ternationalist thinkers off our school boards, out of city
council, and out of our federal and state government.

There is plenty of room in America for secular
humanists who want to live here and enjoy freedom—
in civilian life where they have only an ordinary amount
of influence. It is wrong, however, for us to subsidize
our own national destruction by paying their salary to
make our laws, teach our young, entertain our population, and twist our news. Theirs is a distorted view of
the world and America. They are dangerous when they
have access to the minds of our young!

Tim LaHaye
Author, Educator, Minister

New Age Globalism

**Humanist Agenda for Building
A New World without God**

Contents

Author's Introduction

Secular humanism has many faces. Yet it springs from one fountain—the idea that man doesn't need God.

Out of that corrupt fountain have come the various movements which have disturbed Planet Earth in this century—Socialism, Communism, Fascism, Nazism, and now a movement which I choose to call *New Age Globalism.*

The architects of this movement differ little from those humanists of long ago who undertook to construct the great tower in the Plain of Shinar. It is imperative that their purpose and program be revealed so that those who adhere to a Biblical world-view will be equipped to develop effective counteraction.

The purpose of this book is to draw the attention of pastors, church school teachers, missionaries, church members and American citizens to the existence, strategy, dramatic growth and threatening significance of the globalist movement in our time. It is my prayer that the liberating power of truth will protect our churches, our nation and civilization from the era of tyranny that the architects of New Age Globalism are working diligently to inaugurate.

My wife, Lois, and my secretary, Mrs. Richard Chamberlain, both participated willingly and capably in the typing and finalization of this script, and I thank them sincerely. Also, I am most grateful to George and Norma Swanson for valuable research assistance. It was Norma who first suggested that I undertake this project.

My special thanks goes to that eminent and respected Christian writer, Dr. Tim LaHaye, for responding affirmatively to my suggestion that he write the Foreword to this book.

Finally, it has been a joy to work with Ron Rigsbee, President of Growth Publishing, in connection with production details.

H. Edward Rowe
Washington, D.C.
January, 1985

1
New Age Globalism And Babel

The major issue of our time is the issue of Humanism versus the revealed purpose of God for man.

Humanism is the man-originated and man-centered secular religion which now rises like a tidal wave to put God away and establish the predominance of man within every sphere of life.

The contrast between the God-centered and the man-centered concepts of life is total:

GOD'S WAY	MAN'S WAY
Belief in Centrality of God	Belief in Centrality of man
Rooted in Divine Revelation	Rooted in human reason
God is the Supreme authority	Man is the supreme authority
Theistic	Atheistic
God is the problem-solver	Man is the problem-solver
Freedom is God-given	Freedom is man-made
Man is the product of creation	Man is a product of evolution
Man exists for God	Man exists for himself
Supernaturalistic	Naturalistic
Morality is based on God's Law	Morality is based on man's logic

Salvation is by Divine sacrifice   Salvation is by human science
God is good and man is bad   Man is good and God is bad

The Bible And Humanism

Every era of Biblical history has left behind the unmistakable record of man's drive for predominance. Throughout the ages, "man first" has been the unwritten slogan of the natural man. Always he has devised his schemes for human betterment in total disregard for the clearly revealed will of God.

Without exception, such schemes have failed miserably to solve man's problems. Worse still, they have invariably compounded the very problems which they were intended to solve.

The Creator God has spoken. Individuals who ignore His directives walk in darkness. Institutions and nations which plot their destiny in contempt for the guidelines of Heaven are doomed to experience the spiral descent to decline and failure.

Man at his best, apart from God, will engineer his own doom and dig his own grave. Twenty-two former civilizations, now under the rubble of history, testify loudly to this fact.

Tower Of Babel

A dramatic 6,000 year-old warning concerning the consequences of self conceived human endeavors is sounded in the eleventh chapter of Genesis.

The united families of earth, one in language, speech and purpose, conceived the idea of constructing a tower in the Plain of Shinar. The human purpose is made clear by the text: "... let us build us a city and a tower, whose top may reach unto heaven; and let us make us a name, lest we be scattered abroad upon the face of the whole earth" (Gen. 11:4).

"Lest we be scattered" conveys a perception of the problem of insecurity due to separateness. The human solution was to establish once and for all the primacy and unity of man by building a city, erecting an awe-inspiring tower which would protrude "unto heaven," and thus to make a great and permanent name for a united mankind.

Underlying the entire project was its basic motivation, to which Dr. Merrill F. Unger refers as their "God-defying disobedience and pride."[1] Concerning the expression "whose top may reach unto heaven," Unger comments: "This phrase is not mere hyperbole, but an expression of pride and rebellion manifest by the Babel builders."[2]

The International Standard Bible Encyclopedia concurs, stating that the tower was symbolical of Babylon's pride, since they regarded it as "the house of the foundation of heaven and earth"[3] and dedicated it chiefly to the pagan god Merodach. According to the New Standard Bible Dictionary, Merodach was the "champion of the gods and the supposed savior of the world."[4]

The Babel project conveys a deep meaning for the ages.

Philosophically, it represents belief in the priority of the materialistic realm over the spiritual.

Theolgically, it involves a substitution of false gods for the True and Living God.

Psychologically, it implies confidence in the achievement of security by means of a global man-made unity.

Educationally, it means problem solution based on the adequacy of man rather than the guidance of God.

Administratively, it exhibits an unfounded assurance of the self-sufficiency of organized man without reliance on God.

Anthropologically, it proclaims the glories of human pride and self-aggrandizement.

The outcome of the Babel project is recorded in the sacred text as a warning for all time. The Living God confounded the language of the builders of the city of man—"and from thence did the Lord scatter them abroad upon the face of all the earth" (Gen. 11:9).

We must not miss the central warning that resounds through the corridors of the long centuries to our time. The tower builders structured a mighty global organization, independent of God. They dedicated it to the establishment of a human unity which would secure them against the prospect of being scattered apart throughout the world.

But that which they sought desperately to avoid by means of united human action, actually occurred in spite of their best efforts. The Biblical principle is clear: *The best engineered designs of fallen man will inevitably compound the problem which they are intended to solve.*

So dismal was the failure of the humanist escapade recorded in Genesis 11 that the place where it occurred was named to remind all future generations of what happened there. "Babel" is from the root "balal," which means "to confound."[5]

New Tower Of Babel

The offspring of the Babel builders are with us to this day. Their scheme for constructing a global city of man on planet earth is abundantly evident in their writings.

They intend well, as did the ancient builders. But their good intentions originate with fallen man and ignore the clear guidelines of the Word of God. Therefore, they will succeed no more than did the tower builders of six millennia ago.

The purpose of this book is to examine the *philosophy*, the *religion*, the *values* system and the *strategy* of modern globalism and to lay bare its pagan heart as accurately and vividly as possible, for the benefit of pastors, Christian leaders and laymen everywhere, to the end that the service of all who "seek first the Kingdom of God" (Matt. 6:33) will be enhanced for His glory.

Notes

1. Unger, Merrill F., *Unger's Bible Dictionary*. Chicago: Moody Press, 1969, 1192 pp. Page 114.
2. *Ibid.*, p. 115.
3. Orr, James, Morris O. Evans and Melvin Grove Kyle, Eds., *The International Standard Bible Encyclopedia*. Grand Rapids: Wm. B. Eerdmans Publishing Company, 1952. Five Vols. I, 357.
4. Jacobus, Melancthon W., Edward E. Nourse and Andrew C. Zenos, *A New Standard Bible Dictionary*. New York: Funk & Wagnalls Company, 1926. 965 pp. Page 824.
5. *Op. cit.*, Unger, p. 114.

2
New Age Globalism and Man

An unbridled optimism pervades globalist writings. A new age is fast breaking upon the world. Humanity has an entirely new agenda. There is a whole new set of concepts, communicated by an entirely new vocabulary. A glorious future beckons. Man is at the center.

A New Age

"We are crossing a threshold between our past national awareness and an emerging planetary consciousness," declares an official brochure of *Planetary Citizens*. The statement is buried in a write-up titled "The Great Awakening" in a document featuring headings such as "Human Manifesto" and "Pledge of Planetary Citizenship," and slogans like "One Earth; One Humanity; One Destiny" and "Helping to Unite the Human Family."[1]

The exciting announcement of a marvelous new age pervades globalist literature. Jessica Lipnack and

Jeffrey Stamps begin their mammoth 400-page compendium on "Networking" with the proclamation that "an entirely new culture is emerging in our land."[2] Other writers refer to our time as "this new era in human development"[3] and resort to such labels as "the global era" in order to convey an impression of the wonders that are bursting upon the domain of self-sufficient man.

"Something remarkable is underway," exclaims Marilyn Ferguson in the introduction to her huge book, *The Aquarian Conspiracy.* "It is moving with almost dizzying speed. . . ."[4] Ferguson speaks a great deal about "transformation" and "crossover," by which she has reference to "people changing" through human initiative. Among the globalist communicators, there is not doubt that "our destiny is still in our hands . . . ."[5]

Alvin Toffler sums up the case for the new age on the first page of his best-selling book *The Third Wave:*

> A new civilization is emerging in our lives, and blind men everywhere are trying to suppress it. This new civilization brings with it new family styles; changed ways of working, loving, and living; a new economy; new political conflicts; and beyond all this an altered consciousness as well . . . . The dawn of this new civilization is the single most explosive fact of our lifetime. It is the central event—the key to understanding the years immediately ahead. It is an event as profound as that First Wave of change unleashed ten thousand years ago by the invention of agriculture, or the earthshaking Second Wave of change touched off

by the industrial revolution. We are the children of the next transformation, the Third Wave.[6]

A New Agenda

The "new age" engineered by a new kind of man—the kind who is no longer responsible to God—features its own agenda. Voluminous reading of the globalist "new age" literature brings before the researcher eight major recurring themes which, collectively, constitute the agenda of the movement:

1. The imperative of public funding in order to provide for the betterment of man.

2. The crucial role of the United Nations Organization in forging the unified world of the future.

3. An integrating value system, drawn from the various religious and philosophical approaches to the understanding of reality.

4. The inevitability of progress and the evolution of a near-utopian new world order.

5. Disarmament as the ethical requirement of the new human brotherhood that is being established, and the only road to peace.

6. The building of a global government which will exemplify all the great virtues of the unprecedented planned society of man.

7. The provision of wonderful new alternatives to the traditional family, which now fades into the misty past—a relic of antiquity.

8. Total reliance upon the goodness and wisdom of man for the structuring of the world to come, without any recognition whatever of the Living God of the Hebrew-Christian tradition.

A New Vocabulary

The reader of globalist writings soon finds himself wallowing neck-deep in the peculiar vocabulary of the movement. It is a vocabulary that has been devised by various adherents of the new age concept, in order to communicate its unique features.

An exciting aspect of the globalist experience is the mastering of this futuristic vocabulary. A halo of forward-looking intellectuality surrounds the head of the user. Immediately these far-out words and phrases, like the sounds of another world, arrest the attention of the unaware and arouse curiosity. Quite obviously, a penchant to impress is an integral part of the globalist mentality.

To the extent that they are subject to definition, most of the terms in the globalist vocabulary are self-defining. The following list of terms was encountered while reading globalist literature, and jotted on a note sheet without regard to any order or sequence whatever:

"globalized society"
"global perspective"
"global dimension"
"global education"
"worldmindedness"
"cross cultural contacts"
"global insights"
"deep culture"
"polycultural world"
"global interdependence"

"multicultural education"
"futurology"
"futuristics"
"change management"
"worldwatch"
"transitional perspective"
"intercultural training"
"multinational classroom"
"earthwatch research"
"futures perspective"
"transnational dialogue"
"perspective consciousness"
"planetary citizenship"
"planetary awareness"
"global marketplace"
"global dynamics"
"mundialization"
"planetization"
"age of interdependence"
"intergenerational responsibility"
"ecological self-realization"
"conceptual paradigm shift"
"networking"
"metanetworking"
"networld"
"immersion education"
"transborder data flow"

These are only a few samples of the new vocabulary. Globalists outdo themselves to spin off new han-

dles. They are virtually as numerous as the trees of the forest.

One cannot but muse that the addle-headed rabble that gathered in the Plain of Shinar six millennia ago must have concocted a special vocabulary suitable to the Tower project. Surely they must have displayed their paltry intellects by means of impressive prattlings about the coming new age in which the global life of man would be managed from the man-made heights.

A New Future

The new age of man, with its new agenda and appropriate new vocabulary, is engineering a bright new future. "Planetary culture is the next culture at a quantum leap," explains William Irwin Thompson. "It is not a continuous evolution. It is a quantum leap. So there is a disjunction between these two systems. I am now saying that interntational civilization has reached its limits of growth; something new is coming in, epoch B, conscious cultural evolution of man. This identifies planetary culture."[7]

The vision of the future compares quite favorably with the Old Testament prophetic vision of the coming kingdom—except that the globalist future is to be forged by the hand of man, with no help from God.

The future society of man is heralded glowingly by D.C. Meadows in a statement so pivotal that it heads a chapter in Harold G. Shane's book. *Educating for a New Millennium.*

Affirms Meadows, "Man possesses, for a small moment in his history, the most powerful combination of knowledge, tools, and resources the world has ever known. He has all that is physically necessary to create a totally new form of human society—one that would be built to last for generations."[8]

One must recall the strident voice of a former paperhanger whose confidence in human ingenuity, especially his own, was boundless. In screaming oratory, this twentieth century humanist announced to the world that the Third Reich would establish a new era that would last a thousand years!

America's foundations are of different substance. Benjamin Franklin stated in the Continental Congress that those who would build empires without the concurring aid of God will fail as miserably as did the builders of Babel. Hitler's thousand-year Reich was pounded to bits within a few months, and he shot himself in an undergound hideout.

Needed desperately in our time is not a "quantum leap" into a new epoch contrived by man, who ever fails in his attempts to construct glorious towers and empires, but rather a humble, calculated submission to Almighty God and a return to the founding principles of America. Man's towers soon end in rubble. God's truth is the only foundation on which great nations and civilizations may be constructed.

Notes

1. Promotional brochure of *Planetary Citizens*, 777 United Nations Plaza, New York, N.Y. 10017. (212) 490-2766.

2. Lipnack, Jessica, and Jeffrey Stamps, *Networking: The First Report and Directory*. Garden City, New York: Doubleday & Company, Inc., 1982. 398 pp. Page 1.

3. Kierstead, Fred, Jim Bowman and Christopher Dede, *Educational Futures: Sourcebook I*. Washington, D.C.: World Future Society, 1979. 254 pp. Page viii.

4. Ferguson, Marilyn, *The Aquarian Conspiracy*. Los Angeles: J.P. Tarcher, 1980. 448 pp. Page 18.

5. Mische, Gerald and Patricia, *Toward A Human World Order*. New York: Paulist Press, 1977. 399 pp. Page 361.

6. Toffler, Alvin, *The Third Wave*. New York: William Morrow and Company, Inc., 1980. 516 pp. Page 3.

7. Thompson, William Irwin, on p. 54 of *Emerging Moral Dimensions in Society: Implications for Schooling*, Robert R. Leeper, Ed. Washington: Association for Supervision and Curriculum Development, 1975. 70 pp.

8. Shane, Harold G. with M. Bernardine Tabler, *Educating for a New Millennium*. Bloomington, Indiana: Phi Delta Kappa Educational Foundation, 1981. 160 pp. Page 48.

3
New Age Globalism and Religion

Every movement has some kind of religion as its integrating and motivating principle. Globalism is no exception. It offers a *secular, mystical,* and *universal* religion. Since these three features predominate in globalist religion, we will focus on them in this chapter.

A Secular Religion

The content of the secular religion espoused by globalists is a curious mish-mash of off-beat modern pseudo-psychology and Eastern cult-trips. As Lipnack and Stamps put it:

> "Inner growth, personal change, evolution, transformation. Coming to grips with yourself, changing, growing. Running, practicing yoga and t'ai chi, meditating, sitting, chanting. Consulting astrology, numerology, and the I Ching. Reading the Seth material and the Don Juan books. Alan Watts and Ram Dass. Therapy, rolfing, psycho-

drama, Gestalt, psychosynthesis, bioenergetics, T-groups."[1]

All of these exercises are resorted to by "personal seekers and spiritual aspirants" embarked on a "search for meaning."[2] "Sufi" leader Pir Vilayat Khan identifies this emergent "quest for meaning, for relevance, for coherence" as the "feeling that it all makes sense."[3] The word "feeling" is significant. As we shall see later, human feeling rather than Divine Revelation is the foundational factor is globalist religion.

Globalist literature will be searched in vain for any concept of a transcendent Creator God. Wherever "God" is mentioned, some sort of psychological or mystical encounter is in view. God can be anything from some vague principle of the universe to the "higher Self,"[4] "primordial nature,"[5] or indefinable "process."[6] To one globalist writer, God is "the sum total of consciousness in the universe, expanding through human evolution."[7]

A Mystical Religion

The Berkeley Christian Coalition, an evangelical group which issues analytical reports on anti-Christian movements, has stated that "the mystical worldview" is making "a coordinated thrust into every aspect of our cultural consciousness . . . , and it is fundamentally hostile to Biblical Christianity."[8]

This basic hositility is nowhere more in evidence

than in the idea of the source of truth and knowledge. Christianity is committed to the concept of a Living Creator-God who has revealed Himself to man. God's self-revelation is both through the Living Word (the Person of Christ) and the Written Word (the inspired Scriptures of the Old and New Testaments).

This repository of God's truth constitutes the raw materials from which a theology, a body of doctrine, is formulated by means of the inductive method. To the Christian, a biblically-based doctrinal system is ultimate truth. To know doctrine is to know the mind of the Living God concerning His will for man on Planet Earth.

In contrast, the secular religion of the globalists relies upon mystical experience as the source of "knowledge." From a Christian standpoint, of course, this is heretical. Globalist Marilyn Ferguson recognizes this fact and comments: "Now the heretics are gaining ground, doctrine is losing its authority, and knowing is superseding belief."[9]

In other words, the authoritative Revelation of God to man is being replaced, in this enlightened age, by "direct knowledge" [10] attained through mystical encounters with some source *other* than the God of the Hebrew-Christian tradition. Why be encumbered with "belief," when "direct knowledge," available through mystical guru-encounteres, is far superior to faith?

Christianity and globalist secular religion diverge totally. In scores of instances, Jesus and the New Testament writers demand faith, pure faith unmixed with works, as the only means of access to God. Secular religion pushes faith aside and substitutes mystical "knowledge." Christianity gets its direction from an authoritative doctrinal system, while secular religion despises doctrine and clings to "experiences."

Paul the Apostle warned, " . . . the time will come when they will not endure sound doctrine . . . And they shall turn away their ears from the truth, and shall be turned unto fables."[11] Never were words of Scriptures more prophetically pertinent in relation to a movement than are these words to globalist mystical religion.

Our assessment of globalist religion must ever be rooted in these words of the Apostle John: "Whosoever transgresseth, and abideth not in the doctrine of Christ, hath not God."[12] Let the people of God everywhere be warned: Those who affirm that "The Radical Center of spiritual experience" is "knowing without doctrine"[13] betray thereby that they are not in touch with God.

A Universal Religion

"Universality" is the watchword of the tower builders of Babel. An aura of respectability must belong to those who have risen above the din of divisiveness and petty strife, and are so enlightened as to name as their religious heroes " . . . the Buddha, Jesus, Gandhi, Schweitzer, Teilhard de Chardin, Martin Luther King,

Hammarskjold, U Thant, people who really transcend races, nations, and groups . . . ."[14] These are the people who have "networked at the all-human level, linking the heavens and the earth . . . ."[15]

The passing notice that is given to Jesus, as an "also ran" in the parade of the greats, is significant. The spokesman in this case is Robert Muller, Secretary of the United Nations Economic and Social Council. He wedges the Son of God in between Buddha and Gandhi, thus betraying his open rejection of the Savior's claims of Deity.

This downgrading of the Incarnate God—the One by whom "All things were made"[16]—is characteristic of globalist religious universalism. God is relegated to manhood, and man is elevated to God-like self-sufficiency. This is very much according to the pattern set in the eleventh chapter of Genesis. The tower builders spurned God and projected themselves, through the work of their hands, upward "unto heaven."[17] Their purpose of self-aggrandizement is clear in their rallying cry, " . . . let us make us a name."[18]

In his penetrating book titled *A Study in Syncretism,*" John Cotter quotes the British socialist writer H.G. Wells as affirming that "the coming World-state . . . will be based upon a common World Religion, very much simplified and universalized and better understood."[19] Cotter quotes atheist Julian Huxley as promoting "scientific world humanism, global in extent and evolutionary in background . . . "[20]

21

Writing of globalist religious universalism in general, Cotter summarizes:

> All religions are one in origin and based on a common principle—the spirit of brotherhood. Differences which have arisen are 'accidental' and 'through failure of the followers to understand the Teaching given.' Since no one single religion is capable of meeting the challenge of modern times, so all religions must be merged into a Universal Brotherhood.[21]

Gerald and Patricia Mische see religious universalism as having an impact that far exceeds purely religious purposes. To them, it is a vehicle for forging the new world order:

> Religion-related networks ... provide a unique global fibre for developing the people's coalition for world order. Each religion-related network, through its membership, is in touch with grass-roots people representing all of the other issue constituencies—an 'intouchness' that is growing as many men and women relate themselves full-time to one or more of these issues. Thus a concentration on religion-related networks provides a geometric entree to hundreds of organizations and tens of thousands of creative and initiative-taking men and women dealing with the major issues with which humankind must deal in the final quarter of the twentieth century.[22]

Globalist religion is purely humanistic in conception and secular in its expression. Its derivation is associated with mystical experiences which purportedly bring "direct knowledge" without the need for such encumbrances as antiquated beliefs or doctrinal systems. It welds together the religions of the world in one grand amalgamation of "spiritual" forces intent on forging a new world order. It represents a human attempt, global in scope, to reverse the outcome of the first great effort of man, in the Plain of Shinar, to unite the human family through human schemes.

Globalist religion is man's alternative to God's revealed truth and agelong redemptive plan. In due course, the religion of man will fall under the judgment of the same Living God who "scattered them abroad"[23] from the faltering base of their man-made tower, six millennia ago.

Notes

1. Lipnack, Jessica, and Jeffrey Stamps, *Networking: The First Report and Directory*. Garden City, New York: Doubleday & Company, Inc., 1982. 398 pp. Page 159.
2. *Ibid.*
3. *Ibid.*
4. Satin, Mark, *New Age Politics*. New York: Dell Publishing Company, 1978. 350 pp. Page 129.
5. Ferguson, Marilyn, *The Aquarian Conspiracy*. Los Angeles: J.P. Tarcher, 1980. 448 pp. Page 383.

6. *Ibid.*
7. *Ibid.*
8. *Ibid.*, p. 370.
9. *Ibid.*, p. 371.
10. *Ibid.*, p. 370.
11. 2 Timothy 4:3,4
12. 2 John 9
13. *Op. cit.*, Ferguson, p. 377.
14. *Op. cit.*, Lipnack & Stamps, p. 198.
15. *Ibid.*
16. John 1:3
17. Genesis 11:4
18. *Ibid.*
19. Cotter, John, *A Study In Syncretism.* Flesherton, Ontario: Canadian Intelligence Publications, 1979. 116 pp. Page 2.
20. *Ibid.*
21. *Ibid.*, p. 3.
22. Mische, Gerald and Patricia, *Toward a Human World Order.* New York: Paulist Press, 1977. 399 pp. Pages 305f.
23. Genesis 11:8.

4
New Age Globalism and Values

The *values* held by a movement reflect its assessment of what is right or wrong, desirable or undesirable, worthy or unworthy. The value-system of any movement is based on its religion. Secular religion, of course, contrives its own secular values.

Globalism is guided by a secular value-system that appeals strongly to noble aspirations. Who *wouldn't* want a world without strife and war, poverty, ignorance, discrimination and social turmoil?

The dedicated Christian desires the same end, but he differs from the globalist in a fundamental sense. He knows that human initiative, without that element which Benjamin Franklin referred to as "the concurring aid" of God, is misguided, misplaced, futile and even dangerous.

Dangerous because the humanist tower-builders, in their zeal to implement new and wonderful schemes for world betterment, soon find it necessary to impose tyrannical force in order to press the subjects into their mold.

Lenin's scheme to establish a global millennium, for example, could not go forward except over the corpses of some sixty million victims. Hitler's plan for improving the lot of man was so impressive that secular intellectuals nationwide rushed to his bandwagon—a bandwagon that eventually rolled over and crushed some eighteen million people.

It is the voice of history that the "values" which guide the actions of high-thinking, well-intentioned pagans generally pave the super-highway to disaster. Rather than lead to the solution of human problems, they compound them, resulting in unimagined tragedies and horrors.

Two features of the globalist value system are paramount. It is an emergent value system, and it is a relativistic value system.

An Emergent Value System

While the content of the Christian's value system was conveyed by God through the agency of inspired writers, the humanist-globalist-secular value system has emerged gradually out of the misty past. In the words of Lipnack and Stamps,

> Our human value heritage is deep and wide, rooted in the origin of the planet and life itself, blossoming over the past half billion years of births and deaths. With each new twist of evolution, life acquired new patterns of values to add to the

values already established. The emergence of mortality and sex in simple cell groups, of instinct in reptiles and emotion in mammals, and of tools and speech in the far-distant human generations, have all contributed to our vast value heritage.[1]

What values have thus emerged through the curious convolutions of human development over thousands of millenia? There is an observable "common fabric of values," a "cluster of values,"[2] that have arisen to bless the planetary citizens:

> We are now convinced that there is a vast meganetwork of individual and social change that, in the fuzzy way of networks, maps the territory of an emerging future in America. Its values are healing, sharing, using, valuing, learning, growing and evolving. Three of these values (healing, learning, growing) are oriented to the individual. Three more (sharing, using, evolving) are oriented to the collective. The seventh (valuing) is oriented to the process of human valuing itself.[3]

The mature Christian will detect that certain features of the globalist value system seem to overlap with the Biblical gallery of virtues. Missing, however, are the cardinal New Testament virtues—*faith, hope* and *love* (I Corinthians 13:13). Missing also is the indwelling Holy Spirit who effects actual *change* in the life of the believer, so that values are not merely something to be talked about, but rather to be lived. The aspect of *change* in the life is crucial, and the Apostle Paul refers to it in these words:

But we all, with open face beholding as in a glass the glory of the Lord, are changed into the same image from glory to glory, even as by the Spirit of the Lord.[4]

A Relativistic Value System

A teaching method known as *values clarification* was introduced a couple of decades ago by social scientists Louis E. Raths, Merrill Harmin and Sidney B. Simon. The concept is put forward as an alternative to the worn-out idea of "indoctrinating" students by simply teaching them what is right and what is wrong.

The advocates of values clarification contend that teachers who attempt to convey a Judeo-Christian spectrum of values "manipulate" captive students, "moralizing" and "preaching" to them such rigid standards as are derived from "religion."

It is contended that neither the school nor society has any right to tell students that premarital sex is right or wrong. The teacher should merely assist students in discovering and clarifying their own values, rather than forcing some code of values on them.

Being advocates of ideological humanism, globalists consistently deny that values were written in stone and given to Moses, or otherwise revealed by God. The "New Age perspective," writes Mark Satin, stresses "self-development."[5] Again Satin, in a chapter titled *New Age Ethics and Values*, encourages: "The multidimensional person will want to *develop his or her paths* in many spheres . . . "[6] (italics added for emphasis).

The values clarification paradigm fits with precision the general approach to values that is found in globalist literature: There are no eternal values. All values are relative, and evolving. They originate with man, who alone possesses the power to develop them.

According to an article by Professor Richard A. Baer, Jr., in the *Wall Street Journal*, the "values clarification" technique has been spread around the country by means of teacher workshops, paid for in part by state and federal tax dollars.[7] Inasmuch as its approach to values orientation is virtually identical to that of globalist philosophy, which is, as we shall see later, now running through public education like a prairie fire, tens of millions of our youth will emerge from their formative years in the classroom to go out and face life under the guidance of a relativistic, pagan value system.

The consequences of this massive defection from God-given values can only be tragic for the future of our nation and civilization. Even Chief Justice Warren Burger, whose record in the Supreme Court reflects his own obvious commitment to a relativistic ethic, lamented in a speech in 1981, "We have virtually eliminated from public schools . . . any effort to teach values of integrity, truth, personal accountability and respect for others' rights."[8]

The Builders of old Babel made one basic mistake. They were guided by their own values, rather than

God's. Therefore, God had to take a judgmental hand in their affairs, and their shining tower crumbled. It is a lesson for all time.

Only a return to the Biblical value system that was foundational to education in America from our earliest history, and through most of the nineteenth century, will assure adequate guidance for our nation in the perilous years ahead.

Notes

1. Lipnack, Jessica, and Jeffrey Stamps, *Networking: The First Report and Directory.* Garden City, New York: Doubleday & Company, Inc., 1982. 398 pp. Page 232.
2. *Ibid.,* p. 233.
3. *Ibid.,* pp. 233 f.
4. 2 Corinthians 3:18.
5. Satin, Mark, *New Age Politics.* New York: Dell Publishing Company, 1978. 350 pp. Page 105.
6. *Ibid.,* p. 107.
7. Richard A. Baer, Jr., *Parents, Schools and Values Clarification.* The Wall Street Journal, April 12, 1982.
8. Cited by Terry Eastland in *Teaching Morality in the Public Schools.* The Wall Street Journal, February 22, 1982.

5
New Age Globalism and Evolution

Throughout globalist literature, evolution is taken for granted. In our effort to understand the globalist viewpoint with regard to evolution, we must take note of the meaning, the goal, and the process of evolution within the context of their own writings.

Meaning of Evolution

When the globalist speaks of evolution, he has in view not merely an ages-long passive physiological development of living forms, but rather a radical change for the good that man himself deliberately brings about. What is meant, almost without exception, is an active, rapid, self-induced transformation from the inferior world of the past to the bright new order of the future.

This new twist on evolutionary doctrine is expressed by Lipnack and Stamps:

> Alongside the official pronouncements that evolution happens over many, many lifetimes and is only a series of random mutations . . . is Another

America, which knows in its heart that humanity is evolving very quickly, right now, and that we all are responsible for the outcome.[1]

Dr. William Irwin Thompson, Director of the Lindisfarne Association in Southhampton, Long Island, puts it like this in a small volume titled *Emerging Moral Dimensions in Society:*

> The planetary community opens outward with other groups around the world to effect an evolutionary transformation of human culture. Lindisfarne itself is working with a group in Scotland, a group of scientists in Germany, a Yogic city in India, and a Zen community and farm in California. We are a web that goes around the world.[2]

In his contribution to the same volume, Dr. Jonas Salk of the Salk Institute for Biological Studies in La Jolla, California, announces that his viewpoint is evolutionary, then amplifies:

> As trustees of evolution . . . we ask, what is it that needs to be done or can be done now for the future? A sense that clearly has come about through the evolutionary process exists in man to, you might say, serve his purpose; to serve his purpose simply because it has served the purpose of survival and evolution in the human realm before. Those who have had and exercised foresight have been the ones who have been able to ward off the threats to survival and to the continuation of the evolutionary process.[3]

The concise statement of the meaning of evolution in globalist evolutionary philosophy is that " . . . our responsibility, right now, for the evolution of ourselves and the planet, is inescapable."[4]

In a scheme such as this it is obvious that God is not involved. "Evolutionary transformation" is strictly a function of human foresight, effort and determination. The enlightened among us do not wait for it to happen; they *make* it happen! They are the responsible set—the architects and engineers of the glorious new culture that is evolving.

Goal of Evolution

Progress, conceived in terms of the expanding efforts of humans to realize a developing global unity, is the aim of globalist evolution. According to Dr. Robert Muller, Secretary of the United Nations Economic and Social Council:

> Humanity is evolving toward a coherent global form best described by the metaphor of a human brain; each person, young or old, able-bodied or handicapped, is an important neuron in the emerging planetary brain that is constituted by the myriad 'networkings' among people.[5]

The word *emerging* is employed consistently as the explanation of how the great evolutionary process takes place. As we have seen, man himself is credited with having accomplished his own evolution in past aeons.

Now, man himself is charged with the awesome responsibility of effecting the *emergence* of the unified planet toward which all nature is moving.

There is no explanation beyond man himself. As man develops through naturalistic *emergent* evolution, he causes his culture and his civilization to *emerge* toward a planetary paradise of human cross-cultured unity and caring.

The goal of a better world, free from poverty and strife, is commendable. But six thousand years of history stand as eloquent verification of the Biblical teaching that man, when steering a separate course from God, never fails to compound his difficulties.

To build a tower without God is like building a house upon a foundation of sand (Matt. 7:26–27). Even the most beautiful and sturdy of houses will succumb to the onslaughts of wind and rain. The builder who has operated independently of God is "foolish," as Jesus declared. His folly is evident in the utter failure of his very best purposes to accomplish his own desired ends.

The wise man, on the other hand, builds upon a foundation of solid rock—the will of God. No other foundation—for a life, an institution, a nation or civilization—will endure.

Process of Evolution

The evolutionary process, according to globalists, moves hopefully, juggernaut-like, from age to age, transforming the life and culture of man on Planet Earth, and accelerating in speed. Now, at this exciting time in the ages-long process, a virtual evolutionary explosion, a quantum leap to the indescribable world of tomorrow, is in the offing.

English philosopher Lancelot Law Whyte[6] traces the process from the "nomadic, hunter-gatherer" period, beginning two to five million years ago, through the "neolithic" period to the "Golden Age of Greek thought" and into the "scientific-industrial period" that began with Gutenberg, Kepler, Galileo and Newton and "still dominates the thinking of modern society."[7]

Beginning after World War I, says Whyte, "the signs of the next great transformation in human development first became visible."[8] Predicting that the many threads of change would "rapidly coalesce into a coherent worldview in post-World War II years," Whyte stated that this transition would "probably be complete by the end of the 20th century."[9]

Lipnack and Stamps refer to the "accelerating pace of evolution" and illustrate it by reviewing "the big picture:"[10]

> Life first appeared on earth a billion or so years after the planet's birth almost 5 billion years ago. The bacteria-based bioplanet developed slowly for more than 3 billion years until life exploded in diversity with the coemergence of sex (male and female) and mortality (birth and death) 500 million years ago. Mammals became numer-

ous 75 million years ago. Erect, tool-making primates appeared between 2 and 5 million years ago. Humans settled towns 12,000 years ago. The 'ancient' cultures of Greece and Rome flourished 2,500 years ago. The industrial era is less than 400 years old.[11]

The accelerating pace of the evolutionary process provides the basis of great hope that even a single generation can witness tremendous change for the better:

> Textbook Darwinian theory portrays evolution as slow moving and incremental—a process that 'takes a long time.' Within that worldview it is difficult to imagine that evolution is accelerating, apt to suddenly shift direction, and may indeed be recognizable within the span of a single human life.[12]

The tower-builders in the ancient plain obviously purposed to bless their own generation with the work of their own hands. Their bright idea was to ascend to wonderful new heights of planetary unity through human self-effort.

We can imagine how completely plausible the excellent plan must have appeared, and with what alacrity the populace must have rushed to the support of the new movement. The appeal of a drive to penetrate the heavenly realm and secure the unity of the race must have been electrifying.

But the shining tower, erected on a foundation of sand, was destined to litter the desert. The self-effort of man, in contravention of the will and purpose of

God, was inadequate to effect a quantum leap to the intended bright new age.

The globalist movement of our time, with its pipe-dream of an accelerating evolutionary breakthrough in a single generation, is a new Tower of Babel. It will come to the very same unhappy end as did the Tower of Shinar.

Notes

1. Lipnack, Jessica, and Jeffrey Stamps, *Networking: The First Report and Directory*. Garden City, New York: Doubleday and Company, Inc., 1982. 398 pp. Page 2.
2. *Lindisfarne: Education for a Planetary Culture*, in Leeper, Robert R., *Emerging Moral Dimensions in Society: Implications For Schooling*. Washington, D.C.: Association for Supervision and Curriculum Development, 1975. 72 pp. Page 55.
3. *Ibid.*, pp. 14f.
4. *Op. cit.*, Lipnack and Stamps, p. 243.
5. *Ibid.*, p. 193.
6. *Ibid.*, p. 238.
7. *Ibid.*
8. *Ibid.*
9. *Ibid.*
10. *Ibid.*, p. 243.
11. *Ibid.*
12. *Ibid.*

6
New Age Globalism and Education

If your children are attending a public school, it is highly likely that their teachers will transmit a globalist-humanist-United Nations viewpoint to them.

If that doesn't happen, it will not be due to any lack of intent on the part of the globalist social engineers. They have made no secret of their plans to enter the classrooms of the nation with a full-orbed globalist curriculum. In fact, they regard this as a high duty.

As a Christian and patriotic American, it will be preferable for you to place your children in a school that will uphold the Biblical understanding of life, reality and culture.

If such a school is not available, you will want to insulate your children against Babalism and the false globalist-humanist philosophy. In order to do this, it will be helpful to make yourself aware of the inroads of globalism into education. This chapter will be helpful to that end.

Role of Education

According to a fact sheet which is distributed by the National Education Association (NEA), that organization is "the largest professional organization and the largest public employee organization in the nation."[1] It is claimed that some 90 percent of the NEA's members are classroom teachers, for whom the parent organization negotiates collective bargaining contracts with over 8,500 school systems.

The political viewpoint of NEA is decidedly far to the left of center. It is on record as supporting political tickets such as Carter-Mondale.[2] Also, the NEA openly supports such dubious programs as behavior modification, sex education, population control, the Equal Rights Amendment (which still is not dead), decriminalization of marijuana, a cabinet level office of education, federal day-care centers, public welfare, national health insurance, teacher strikes, school busing, etc.

In addition to this left-wing agenda, the NEA strongly supports other expressions of secular humanism, including the United Nations and an active program to construct a new global society.

In June, 1976, the NEA's former presidents and then current chairmen of its Bicentennial Committee commented as follows concerning educators and their role in relationship to the developing new world order or global community:

It is with ... sobering awareness that we set about to change the course of American education for the twenty-first century by embracing the ideals of global community, the equality and inter-dependence of all peoples and nations, and education as a tool to bring about world peace.[3]

The NEA, then, perceives education as a vehicle for capturing the minds of our school children and, through them, building the planned new globalist society of Planet Earth.

In harmony with this scheme, the National Council for the Social Studies conducts professional meetings in which the "global perspective" is advocated among curriculum planners. One such meeting was convened November 14–21, 1981, in Detroit, on the occasion of the sixty-first Annual Meeting of the National Council for the Social Studies. Dorothy I. Seaberg, Professor of Education in the Department of Curriculum and Instruction at Northern Illinois University, DeKalb, presented a paper titled *Social Systems: Paradigm for a New Social Studies with a Global Perspective.*

In this meticulously written 24-page scholarly paper, Seaberg stressed the need to "chart new directions" consistent with "the nature and purpose of the social studies:"[4]

Through a transdisciplinary view, the social studies interrelates all of the disciplines or systems of knowledge and shows the interconnections involved in the global or world system—in other words, the systemness inherent in the universe. Within the community of social educators, there is a growing consensus that the purpose of the social studies is to educate for participatory citizenship within the global system.[5]

Seaberg goes on to urge social science curriculum professionals and teachers to take an active hand in "bettering the world" by moving "away from nationalistic and ethnocentric perspectives to a global view when analyzing issues and making decisions."[6]

Globalist literature bubbles and fizzes with statements to the effect that "educators should facilitate alternative societal directions."[7] It is largely through *education* that "a whole variety of known quantum jumps of an evolutionary/revolutionary nature"[8] must take place. "The assumption . . . that human beings are unable to understand and powerless to control their world must be abandoned."[9]

Educators who would be involved in the task of "inventing the educational future" must have "faith in the capacity of human intelligence to comprehend the world and control its destiny."[10] The "capacity of education to nurture a broadly based humanism"[11] must be realized. Knowledge should point the way "toward the goal of the rehabilitation of the human will and the rebirth of faith and confidence in the human person."[12]

Expressed in a very few words which go the heart of the matter, "education must be an agent of cultural change."[13] That is the *role* of education as globalists see it.

Content of Education

Having taken note of the globalist definition of the *role* of education as a mighty agent for changing the world in accordance with their planetary dream, let us look at the means whereby they are now undertaking to accomplish this. In a word, they plan to do it by controlling the *content* of education—through curriculum engineering.

Kirschenbaum and Simon want to set in motion "schoolwide curricular reorganization along humanistic lines."[14] This they would accomplish in three ways:

> 1. by incorporating humanistic education approaches into presently existing courses;
> 2. by creating new courses with a specific focus on some aspect of humanistic education;
> 3. by reorganizing the whole school, or major parts of it, to allow for humanistic approaches.[15]

The scheme of the globalist educational elite to accomplish their goals by manipulating the curriculum is dramatized in a book by Harold G. Shane titled *Educating for a New Millennium*. The book summarizes the wisdom of 132 international scholars concerning ways and means of manipulating the student mind and harnessing this resouce for the launching of the coming wonderful man-made millennium.

The contents of the volume reflect the best speculations of an in-group, intellectually in-bred by a system that orbits around man. The viewpoint is consistently globalist, and there is not the slightest gravitational pull toward God, Theology, the Bible, or anything spiritual. The whole idea is to "explore the interaction between curriculum development and societal change,"[16] and to bring about the desired movement toward the dreamed-of millennial splendor.

Nowhere is the Babalist scheme to catapult the world forward into the globalist new-age era of planetary citizenship and interdependent transcultural wonders stated with greater clarity and force than in a small book published in 1978 by the United Nations Association of the United States of America under the title *Helping Boys and Girls to Discover the World*. The subtitle is *Teaching about Global Concerns and the United Nations in Elementary and Middle Schools.*

"Girls and boys growing up today have a right and a need to realize that they are part of an amazing, totally new development in human history,"[17] says Jean Picker, Vice Chairman of the publishing association in the introduction. Further, she announces boldly that " . . . at the United Nations work is underway to forge a global community able to meet the challenges of the next century."[18]

The globalist outlook "must become a part of a child's attitudes and values at the earliest possible age,"[19] writes Picker, who amplifies as follows:

> A global dimension should be given to all subjects and to many other school experiences. Children in the early grades should *learn about the*

ideals of the United Nations and its widespread work to help people better their lives. Affective and active methods should be used which will involve pupils. *Education itself should be profoundly changed* (emphasis added).[20]

This UNA volume features an unbroken stream of propaganda for the United Nations as the great bright hope for the creation of "a new kind of human being" through "a new type of education."[21] British educator Herbert Read is quoted as calling for "a complete recasting and reorientation of our educational system," by which he means "a complete transformation of the aims and methods of education."[22]

Some features of the new education that will create a new type of human being are the following:

1.   introduction of school children to the U.N. flag[23]

2.   observance of United Nations Day as an international holiday[24]

3.   the holding of a birthday party for the U.N.[25]

4.   participation by children in UNICEF Trick or Treat programs at Halloween[26]

5.   simple explanation of the U.N. when children hear about it on television[27]

6.   conveying information about the U.N.'s Universal Postal Union which helps get letters from one part of the world to another[28]

7.   description of some of the things the U.N. is doing to protect the water of the world[29]

8.   teaching about the U.N.'s related agencies[30]

9.   giving the children a unit of teaching on the U.N. system itself[31]

10.   holding up as examples the heroes of the U.N. such as Count Bernadotte and Dag Hammarskjold

11.   observance of World Health Day, World Environmental Day, U.N. Day and U.N. Week[32]

12.   collection of stamps issued by the U.N.[33]

13.   study of outstanding U.N. documents such as the U.N. Charter, the Universal Declaration of Human Rights, the Preamble to the Constitution of UNESCO, etc.[34]

14.   formation of a UNESCO or U.N. club[35]

15.   presentation of a U.N. program for a school assembly[36]

Many and varied are the methods suggested by UNA in this book for altering the actual curriculum content of schools everywhere, in order to glorify the U.N. as the architect of the coming new world order conceived and implemented by man, without any help from God. There are "eight objectives"[37] of a model school curriculum, "13 themes to stress in schools anywhere in the world,"[38] and "our list of 35 books" which includes "volumes we like and have discovered that children like."[39] Impressive lists of films and film strips are also featured.[40]

A profusion of courses, workshops, conferences, symposiums, forums, conventions, etc., are available to school teachers and administrators who wish to sharpen their professional ability to enhance curriculum modification for the accomplishment of globalist goals.

"Global Perspectives in Education" is the name of a New York organization which works actively for the implementation of the globalist agenda and curriculum in educational circles. The organizaiton publishes a newsletter called *Global Perspectives*, which regularly features a calendar of happenings.

One issue of the newsletter displays a two-page splash headlined "32 Ways to Have a Global Summertime."[41] As the heading suggests, the listing includes summer programs nationwide which inform the teacher and administrator as to where and when he or she may develop greater competence in the art of helping to build the global society through education.

The reader of globalist books and other literature is left with no room for doubt that public education is being seized upon as the primary change-agent to fashion the new globalist world, and that the program to accomplish this features curriculum engineering.

It is a grand scheme. The tower builders will use our school children as their bricks in constructing their shining new-age tower. But as we have seen, the builders of the tower have bypassed God. Their language of a new global day projects a noble-sounding concept, and many rush to it. But without the wisdom and aid of God, the bricks will be scattered in the plain.

That is a frightening prospect when you consider that your child might be one of the bricks.

Notes

1. Cited in *Education For a New World Order,* by Michael Loyd Chadwick, Editor, Freeman Digest, September, 1978, p. 1.
2. *Ibid.*
3. From the Foreword to *A Declaration of Interdependence: Education for a Global Community, A Summary Report of the NEA Bicentennial Program.* NEA publication dated June 26, 1976.
4. Seaberg, Dorothy I., *Social Systems: Paradigm for a New Social Studies with a Global Perspective.* Unpublished paper issued by Dorothy I Seaberg, Professor of Education, Department of Curriculum and Instruction, Northern Illinois University, DeKalb, Illinois 60115. Page 1.
5. *Ibid.,* p. 2.
6. *Ibid.*
7. Kierstead, Fred, Jim Bowman and Christopher Dede, *Educational Futures:* Sourcebook I. Washington, D.C.: World Future Society, 1979. 254 pp. Page 3.
8. *Ibid.,* p. 4.

9. *Ibid.*, p. 60.
10. *Ibid.*
11. Mische, Gerald and Patricia, *Toward A Human World Order*. New York: Paulist Press, 1977. 399 pp. Page 216.
12. Illich, Ivan, *Deschooling Society*. New York: Harper & Row, Publishers, 1971, 181 pp. Page 174.
13. Shane, Harold G. and June Grant, *Educating the Youngest for Tomorrow*. Chapter eleven in Toffler, Alvin, Ed., *Learning For Tomorrow*. New York: Vintage Books (A Division of Random House), 1974. 421 pp. Page 183.
14. Kirschenbaum, Howard, and Sidney B. Simon, *Values and the Futures Movement in Education*. Chapter fifteen in Toffler, Alvin, Ed., *Learing For Tomorrow*. New York: Vintage Books (A Division of Random House), 1974. 421 pp. Page 269.
15. *Ibid.*, p. 267.
16. *Op. cit.*, Shane, p. 74.
17. Kenworthy, Leonard S., Ed., *Helping Boys and Girls Discover the World*. United Nations Association of the United States of America, 1978. 74 pp. Page 1.
18. *Ibid.*
19. *Ibid.*
20. *Ibid.*
21. *Ibid.*, p. 4.
22. *Ibid.*
23. *Ibid.*, p. 6.
24. *Ibid.*

25. *Ibid.*
26. *Ibid.*
27. *Ibid.*
28. *Ibid.*, p. 7.
29. *Ibid.*
30. *Ibid.*
31. *Ibid.*
32. *Ibid.*
33. *Ibid.*
34. *Ibid.*
35. *Ibid.*
36. *Ibid.*
37. *Ibid.*, p. 14.
38. *Ibid.*
39. *Ibid.*, p. 62.
40. *Ibid.*, pp. 66–69.
41. "32 Ways to Have a Global Summertime." *Global Perspectives*, 218 E. 18 St., New York, NY 10003. April/May, 1981, pp. 14f.

7
New Age Globalism and the Family

Those who are committed to the humanist-globalist orientation are generally characterized by a godless consistency. Just as they have left God out of their view of man, religion, values and education, they ignore God within the orbit of family life.

This is serious, since the family is the basic unit of society. To disregard Biblical directives for the family is to pave the highway to doom for nations and civilizations. The undermining of the very foundations of a society is bound to set in motion an accelerating momentum toward its collapse.

Marriage Becoming Obsolete

"Citizen of the Universe" F.M. Esfandiary, author of books titled *Up-wingers*, *Optimism One* and *Telespheres*, and a teacher at New York's New School For Social Research, believes the "thrust of history and evolution is incontrovertible and inrreversible." A significant component of his prophetic vision relates to *marriage,* which, he says, is becoming obsolete. He paints his dream in these words:

> Social structures will be revolutionized, with such institutions as marriage and the family becoming obsolete. Children will be produced at the direction of geneticists, after careful matching of superior sperm and egg cells. Fertilization and gestation will occur outside the body. Exclusive parenthood will become a thing of the past. Children will have many parents. They will be raised in communalities, where people who want to share in parenting will go. Marriage and other such exclusive relationships will disappear, to be replaced by a multiplicity of options.[1]

While Esfandiary is one of the more innovative of the globalist-futurist writers, his viewpoint concerning the outlook for marriage and the family is quite typical. His prediction of a "multiplicity of options" prompts a query as to what globalists have in mind.

This will become apparent as we turn now to an important book written for teachers and published by the National Council For The Social Studies in 1975. The book is titled *Controversial Issues in the Social Studies: A Contemporary Perspective.* In the Foreword to the book, Jean Tilford, President of the National Council for the Social Studies, affirms that teachers must "face up to controversy" and "teach students *how* to think, not *what* to think."[2]

Alternatives to Marriage

Professor Esfandiary's reference to the "multiplicity of options" which are destined to replace the "exclusive relationships" of archaic marriage forms leads us to a review of the various life styles which are listed by John F. Cuber, Martha Tyler John and Kenrick S. Thompson in the third chapter of the "Controversial Issues" book.

This 34-page chapter is titled *Should Traditional Sex Modes and Values Be Changed?* The authors refer to the traditional Judeo-Christian marriage-and-family lifestyle as the "monolithic code" which, they say, consisted of the following tenets:

1. The correct adult mode of life was marriage.
2. Marriages are for keeps.
3. Sexual conduct was to be limited to the married state.
4. Marriages should be fruitful.
5. Parents should be responsible . . . and children should be obedient.
6. Women's place was in the home.
7. There was a sharp division of labor between men and women in the home and out, and the power to make and enforce decisions rested primarily, if not exclusively, with the husband.[3]

"As everyone knows, the monolithic code, nestled in history, is in the eyes of many contemporaries archaic—or worse," the authors observe. It was, after all, a "totally sexist ideology."[4] Furthermore, it is now being "challenged" and, as a result, is appropriately styled "the crumbling code."[5]

Evidence of this "crumbling" is seen in the upsurge of "alternate life styles,"[6] of which no less than a dozen are mentioned:

1. *Consensual Unions* (couple simply *consenting* to live together without bothering to marry)

2. *Open Marriages* (winking at adulterous relationships practiced by a partner in marriage who finds "monogamous life-long marriage with clear sex role differentiations simply too repressive" and is "ill-adjusted to monogamy")

3. *Swinging* (parties in which "married couples meet" and "it is understood that each spouse has sexual access during the party to others than his or her spouse")

4. *Communes* (several males and females living together with "the expectation . . . that sexual access is free")

5. *Co-Marital Sex* (legitimate extramarital relationships in which married people do not wish to terminate their marriage, but "who wish at the same time to have additional intimate relationships")

6. *Childless Marriage* (cases where married

people feel they are "not good parent material" or consider children "inimical to the occupational and recreational life styles which many urban people opt to follow")

7. *Subcontracting Parenthood* (reliance on "parent surrogates of numerous kinds," such as child care centers)

8. *Abortion Reform* ("Abortion is, after all, essentially an extension of the contraceptive idea . . . .")

9. *Unisex* (elimination of sex role differences)

10. *Gay Liberation* (legitimation of homosexuality and "agitation for homosexual marriages between consenting adults" are cited as examples)

11. *Bi-Sexuality* (expression of one's sexuality "with either sex")

12. *Women's Liberation* ("abolition of sexist thinking and policy with regard to employment, morality, lifestyle and etiquette, abortion reform, expansion of day care center facilities, and so on")

Implications for the Classroom

Cuber, John and Thompson are teachers of teachers. Their writings in this book are expressions of professional educational philosophers, and are published for the consumption of teachers and administrators in our public schools. It is important, therefore, to take special note as to whether they take any position concerning the morality or immorality of the dozen "alternative life styles" which they enumerate and describe.

The answer is not far to be sought. Schools deal with young people who are "beginning to identify themselves as unique human beings." They must be led by their teachers to "come to terms with plurality and change in society," in order that they might develop a "strong, positive image of themselves as individuals."[7]

The conclusion of the matter is stated as follows:

> The school can provide information on any or all of these variables and in so doing may help the individual build a positive self-concept.[8]

Amplification is provided only a few pages later:

> How then shall young people be prepared to deal with a society in which individual sex identification, the relationship of one individual to another as sexual beings, and the broadening of behaviors appropriate to a given sex role are all undergoing scrutiny and change? It seems clear that strategies must be provided that allow the student to select, develop, and process a topic *in the manner that the individual student deems most appropriate* (emphasis added).[9]

With regard to all of the grossly immoral life styles listed, then, these mentors of public school teachers recommend that the various alternatives be presented to the students. Let the students themselves take the lead in selecting and developing such topics, once the teacher has provided information on "any or all of these variables."[10]

Interestingly, the traditional Judeo-Christian life style is not included in the list of options to be presented to students. In fact, it is disparaged as "totally sexist," and "archaic—or worse."

Obviously, these purveyors of humanist ideology do not believe the teachings of the Word of God concerning sex, marriage and the family are good for the "self-concept" of students. In their perception of reality, the "*self*-concept" is all important and any idea of a "*God*-concept" is nonexistent.

Changing Perception of Morals

Nowhere is the globalist-humanist defection from Biblical guidelines more visible than in its rejection of sex-related morals. An example is found in a chapter titled *The Renewal of Humankind* in a small book by Professor Theodore Brameld presented under the title *The Teacher As World Citizen—A Scenario of the 21st Century*. This volume was published in 1976 by ETC Publications.

The Foreword, written by Jack R. Frymier, Editor of the Educational Forum, states that the book is a part of the "Kappa Delta Pi Lecture Series" which was in-

itiated in 1929 by John Dewey. In this book, says
Frymier, Professor Brameld "has described in detail
the kind of world he hopes we will be able to achieve
by the year 2000."

Brameld speaks of "innumerable signs of rapid
familial evolution"[11] as a hopeful feature of his scenario
of the future. One of these "signs" is a "feature of
human renewal"[12] which he calls "the Age of Eros."
He comments:

> In any event, most of the taboos that had
> warped the lives of countless millions have been
> quite as rapidly dissolving in the erotic dimension
> as they have in family living as a whole. Despite
> stubborn resistance, especially from institutions
> still governed by medieval religious beliefs, the
> new world order embraces most emphatically the
> *humanistic*—in this case, a philosophy centering,
> not in the negation, but rather in the *affirmation*
> of human life in all its infinite range of capacities.
> Sexuality is, of course, precious to this affirmation.
> Rather than stunting or denying its satisfactions,
> every yea-saying celebration of Eros encourages
> them to the utmost.[13]

Extolling the virtues of the Age of Eros, Brameld
discusses more directly the "adventurous" aspects of
the new family concept:

> Returning to marriage and the family . . . it
> follows as a matter of course that the Age of Eros
> is itself dynamic and adventurous. One of the
> cruelest devices of our inherited civilization was,

> I think, the notion that marriage must continue
> 'until death do us part,' even though it sometimes
> meant a living death of hypocrisy, jealousy, and
> incompatability. When marriages do afford satis-
> faction and stability, let us by all means condone
> them. I myself, it happens, have remained mar-
> ried for about two decades because Kimo and I
> enjoy living together, erotically as well as socially
> and professionally. But I have never expected him
> to remain 'faithful' if, at any time, he finds a
> woman or man sufficiently interesting to venture
> an erotic relationship, nor does he expect me to
> do so.[14]

Professor Brameld goes on to condone "successive marriages,"[15] "divorce by common consent," "abortion freely available to both the married and unmarried," and "erotic deviances among consenting adults."[16]

Brameld then praises Marcuse's term "polymorphous perversity," a "fancy term for the varieties of sexual experience—to be infinitely preferred to the perversities of denial and shame that sickened the moral turpitude of our ancestors."[17]

The foundation of the new Tower of Babel is firmly set in the unrealiable sands of immorality. In their view of marriage and the family, the Babel builders join their voices with the anti-God social engineers of Psalm Two who declared, "Let us break their bands assunder, and cast away their cords from us."

The bands and cords of the Almighty are too restrictive. Needed, claim the Babalists, is a great new

"Age of Eros" in which unshackled man will express himself in accordance with the directives of the flesh rather than those of the Word of God.

Notes

1. The citations from F.M. Esfandiary are taken from an article titled *Among Futurists, A Prophet of Boom,* by Leslie Bennetts. New York Times, July 11, 1979.
2. Muessig, Raymond H., Ed., *Controversial Issues in the Social Studies: A Contemporary Perspective.* Washington, D.C.: National Council for the Social Studies, 1975. 308 pp. Page ix.
3. *Ibid.,* p. 91.
4. *Ibid.*
5. *Ibid.,* p. 93.
6. *Ibid.,* pp. 97–102.
7. *Ibid.,* p. 104.
8. *Ibid.*
9. *Ibid.,* p. 107.
10. *Ibid.,* p. 104.
11. *The Renewal of Humankind.* Chapter IV of Brameld, Theodore, *The Teacher As World Citizen.* Palm Springs: ETC Publications, 1976. 83 pp. Page 41.
12. *Ibid.,* p. 44.
13. *Ibid.,* p. 45.
14. *Ibid.,* pp. 45 f.
15. *Ibid.,* p. 46.
16. *Ibid.,* p. 47.
17. *Ibid.,* p. 48.

8
New Age Globalism and Government

Globalists look to the emergence of some form of world government to save the planet from nuclear destruction and usher in the new age of peace and plenty.

The world supergovernment concept is the political arrangement for implementing the globalists' ideology and achieving their far-reaching goals. Universal government is the capstone of the entire globalist scheme.

Just as the ancient builders envisioned a tower "whose top may reach unto heaven" (Gen. 11:4), their modern offspring dream of a vast planetary government with man in control.

The entire evolutionary dream of a transformed world finds its fulfillment and permanence in such an outcome. World government is the ultimate mechanism toward which all globalist aspirations move.

The Underlying Ideology

The atheist-socialist philosopher Bertrand Russell

summed up the case for world government in one sentence:

> Science has made unrestricted national sovereignty incompatible with human survival. The only possibilities are now world government or death.[1]

Another professed atheist, Isaac Asimov, in a Chicago Tribune interview printed on August 1, 1976, was asked whether there can be "world powers" in the year 2000. His reply is summarized as follows:

> We will be living in a global economy; we will be trying to solve global problems by finding global solutions; and behind all the surface blather that will continue the pretense of life in a 20th Century congeries of nations, we will be approaching a 21st Century Global Government.[2]

Lord Beveridge of England put it this way:

> World peace requires world order. World order requires world law. World law requires world government.[3]

Globalists see the nation-state as obsolete. In the words of Hans J. Morgenthau, the nation-state "has been rendered obsolete by the nuclear revolution in the same way in which feudalism was made obsolete 200 years ago . . . . "[4]

In *The Third Wave*, Alvin Toffler discusses the rise of the new globalist ideology:

> Just as the Second Wave created a slice of the

population that had larger than local interests and became the base for nationalist ideologies, so the Third Wave gives rise to groups with larger than national interests. These form the base of the *emerging globalist ideology* sometimes called 'planetary consciousness.'

This consciousness is shared by multinational executives, long-haired environmental campaigners, financiers, revolutionaries, intellectuals, poets, and painters, not to mention members of the Trilateral Commission. I have even had a famous U.S. four-star general assure me that 'the nation-state is dead.' Globalism presents itself as more than an ideology serving the interests of a limited group. Precisely as nationalism claimed to speak for the whole nation, globalism claims to speak for the whole world. And its appearance is seen as an evolutionary necessity—a step closer to a 'cosmic consciousness' *that would embrace the heavens as well* (emphasis added).[5]

Professor Robert Heilbroner laments that he must tell his students that they must belong to "some kind of nation-state," and explains: "At the same time, I feel that nation-states are one of the great curses of history, and that socioeconomic systems are, by and large, all dreadful."[6]

It is abundantly clear that globalists view the nuclear threat and the issue of war and peace, along with problems relating to energy, poverty, food shortages, raw materials, air and water pollution, human rights, overpopulation, environmental deterioration, etc., as of such scope and magnitude as to demand the development of a man-made central controlling mechanism which will protect man from self-destruction.

They reason that if government can be a workable arrangement at the national level, some kind of super-government can be effective at the international level. World government is a pragmatic necessity if man is to survive.

The U.N. As Foundation

In *New Age Politics*, Mark Satin rejects the concept of a "monolithic world government" and prefers instead a coming "planetary guidance system."[7] In writing about the structure of such a system, Satin asserts: "Probably most planetarians see it as an outgrowth of the U.N."[8] He adds: Certainly few planetarians would deny that the U.N. mirrors the actual state of the world's readiness to cooperate . . . . "[9]

As Satin suggests, the United Nations is very much in focus when globalists think about the structure of the evolving world order. After all, says Satin, the U.N. has for some time now been establishing a series of "departments of planetary management in the fields of health, education, agriculture, energy, economic development, population, and environment."[10]

The emerging pattern seems to call for "a system of interrelated departments each with its own area of competence and mechanisms for governance, as well as a system of representation from the world community. They will remain ultimately responsible to the main Organs of the United Nations—the General Assembly and the Security Council."[11]

This dream of a centralized world authority, variously referred to as *third force politics, enlightened humanism, global humanism, radical humanism, synergic politics, participatory divinity* and *New Age Politics*,[12] revolves around the U.N. as its foundational entity. Elaborate structural schemes of various kinds are described, but all superstructures will rise upon the foundation of the U.N.

World Order Structures

Upon the already existing foundation—the United Nations—globalists propose to construct various types of authority systems. Opinions differ as to the best way to structure the new world order system.

One opinion is being put forward by the World Federalists Association. The basic idea is stated simply: Texas and California do not go to war against each other because they both belong to a federal system—the U.S. government—which keeps this from happening. That being the case, the various nations of the world would likewise be restrained from open hostilities against one another if they each belonged to a worldwide federal system.

The platform of the World Federalists contains the following planks:

- granting the U.N. the authority to make laws, binding on individuals as well as governments, to enforce disarmament and to provide for the orderly resolution of disputes between nations.
- conferring on a world judiciary the final authority to interpret these laws and to try individuals accused of violating them.
- creating a system of inspectors and world police to enforce these laws.
- granting authority to the U.N. legislative body to raise reliable revenues under a carefully defined taxing power.
- providing a schedule for universal and complete disarmament.
- establishing a World Development Authority which would be provided with the resources needed to promote the economic and social advancement of the less developed nations.[13]

In their book *Toward A Human World Order*, Gerald and Patricia Mische include a 35-page chapter titled "On Conceiving a New World Order" (chapter 9)[14] and a 52-page chapter titled "Strategies for a Just World Order" (chapter 10).[15] They list eight premises underlying their approach to the structuring of a world order.

These include human ability to choose a preferred world, the need for physical survival, the wisdom of building on "specialized U.N. agencies," a nonideological problem-solving framework, shared sovereignty, and transnational-transcultural participation.

Under such a scheme, man depends totally on his own resources. The tower builders of Shinar set the example six millennia ago: " . . . let *us* build *us* a city and a tower, whose top may reach unto heaven; and let *us* make *us* a name . . . . " (Gen. 11:4)

"Nonideological" problem solving certainly means that Biblical principles, which the Christian must accord the primary place in problem solving, would be excluded altogether. Man, who has made a mess of his own affairs throughout recorded history, sets out once again to build his tower without God.

Gerald and Patricia Mische go on to report on the "World Order Models Project,"[16] a service of the *Institute for World Order.* Eight teams of "scholars from every major area of the world" have been brought together "in a transnational and multicultural effort"[17] to design the structure of world government.

The respective teams are planning various "models" of the future, complete with "functional agencies"[18] to control the seabed, global communications, science and technology, outer space, world ecological balance, financing for development, and transnational corporations. It is stated, hopefully, that the "infrastructure" of such a setup is "already in place and developing."[19]

The long shadow of the Tower of Babel falls across the landscape of this twentieth century. Man has failed to learn from the dramatic episode in the ancient Plain. God spoke, but man did not hear.

The lessons of the distant past, which God has

preserved for our guidance, are disregarded. Man is determined to build a new world without God. It must, of course, fail as miserably as did the Babel project.

> For other foundation can no many lay than
> that is laid, which is Jesus Christ (I Cor. 3:11).

In the next chapter, we will examine the ideological foundation upon which the modern globalist Tower of Babel has been constructed.

Notes

1. Quoted in an official brochure of the World Federalists Association, titled World Federalists Association ... *World Peace Through World Law With Justice ... Developing New Avenues to World Order.* 1101 Arlington Blvd., Suite S-119, Arlington, Va 22209.
2. Chicago Tribune, August 1, 1976, Section 2.
3. *Parliamentarians for World Order,* by Phillip D. Butler. The Canadian Intelligence Service, Vol. 33, No. 5. May 1983. p. 41.
4. Speech by Hans J. Morgenthau at Pacem in Terris Convocation, February, 1965.
5. Toffler, Alvin, *The Third Wave.* New York: William Morrow and Company, Inc., 1980. 516 pp. Page 308.
6. *Education for Alternative Lifestyles,* by Robert Heilbronner, New School for Social Research. Included

in Leeper, Robert R., Ed., *Emerging Moral Dimensions In Society: Implications For Schooling.* Washington, D.C.: Association for Supervision and Curriculum Development, 1975. 70 pp. Page 33.

7. Satin, Mark, *New Age Politics.* New York: Dell Publishing Company, 1978. 350 pp. Page 150.
8. *Ibid.,* p. 151.
9. *Ibid.*
10. *Ibid.*
11. *Ibid.* Here Satin quotes Donald Keys, President of Planetary Citizens.
12. *Ibid.,* p. 9.
13. *Op. cit.,* Butler, p. 41.
14. Mische, Gerald and Patricia, *Toward A Human World Order.* New York: Paulist Press, 1977. 399 pp. Pages 241–76.
15. *Ibid.,* pp. 277–329.
16. *Ibid.,* p. 247.
17. *Ibid.,* p. 248.
18. *Ibid.,* p. 249.
19. *Ibid.*

9
New Age Globalism and Ideology

There are only two movements in history—God's and man's. These two movements are founded on contrary ideologies.

God's movement has been revealed in the Holy Scriptures, which tell us about salvation through Christ, freedom, morality, justice, and the life of service. It is theocentric: God is at the center.

Man's movement is humanism. It is based on the denial of God's existence. It is anthropocentric: Man is at the center.

God's movement is God working for man—saving and uplifting him. Man's movement is man working for man—in contravention of God-given guidelines for human conduct.

The Bible teaches that God has given us the spiritual wisdom with which we may build a healthy and useful life, organization, or nation.

Humanism assumes that man knows best. It brushes aside the wisdom of God. It depends on human thought processes for the solution of all problems. Having cut itself off from the only reliable source of light and wisdom, it always leads men to confusion and darkness.

Humanism is the godless, groundless secular religion which underlies the warped and dangerous thinking behind much of the social activism of our time. It is satanic in origin. It represents man's effort to solve his problems and shape his society apart from God. It is exactly the opposite of true Christianity, which seeks the guidance of the Word of God for the solution of human problems.

Creed of Humanism

The official creed of humanism was until recently expressed in the *Humanist Manifesto*, which was published in *The New Humanist* in 1933. This document boldly denied the creatorship of God, stating that man has "emerged as the result of a continuous process." Man's religious culture and civilization are the product of "a gradual development due to this interaction with his natural environment and with his social heritage." Modern science " . . . makes unacceptable any supernatural or cosmic guarantees of human values."

According to the *Manifesto*, the time has passed for belief in God. The purpose of man's life is "the complete realization of human personality." All associations and institutions "exist for the fulfillment of human life." A better life for man can only be found through "a socialized and cooperative economic o' must be established "to the end that the eq tribution of the means of life" will be assureu. Humanists, says the *Manifesto*, "demand a shared life in a shared world."

Heart of Humanism

Since this so-called *Manifesto* first appeared in 1933, various intellectual humanists have become increasingly aware of its inadequacy. Paul Blanshard, author of the book *American Freedom and Catholic Power,* is a humanist thought leader and contributor to the pages of *The Humanist*. In 1973 he took part in a forum sponsored by that journal for the purpose of establishing the need to revise and update the *Humanist Manifesto* of 1933. Blanshard wrote as follows:

> ... We have an obligation to expose and attack the world of religious miracles, magic, Bible-worship, salvationism, heaven, hell, and all the mythical deities. We should be particularly specific and energetic in attacking such quack millennialists as Billy Graham and such embattled reactionaries as Pope Paul VI because they represent the two greatest anti-humanist aggregates in our society.
> *The Humanist,* March-April, 1973

This statement by Paul Blanshard summarizes the true heart of the humanist position—its rejection of the Bible, Christ, and salvation.

The New *Manifesto*

In September of 1973, the American Humanist Association, acting jointly with the American Ethical Union, released the final text of *Humanist Manifesto II*. This document proved to be far more than a mere revision of the 1933 *Manifesto*. The 1973 statement represents an entirely new effort to express the philosophy of humanism to a world still groaning under the burdens which *Manifesto I* had failed to alleviate in the past four decades.

The full text of *Humanist Manifesto II* should be studied carefully by any reader who wishes to gain objective insight into the nature, purpose, and direction of the contemporary humanist movement. The document is upwards of four thousand words in length. It consists of a preface, an introduction and seventeen points organized under six major headings: Religion, Ethics, The Individual, Democratic Society, World Community, and Humanity as a Whole. The names of 114 signers, among whom are nine Unitarian ministers, two rabbis, and two professors of religion, are appended to the statement.

The preface states that "It is forty years since *Humanist Manifesto I* (1933) appeared." Events since then make that earlier statement seem "far too optimistic." The past forty years have witnessed Nazism, inhuman wars, police states, unyielding racism, poverty, and other evils. An "affirmative and hopeful vision" is needed as we approach the twenty-first century.

Humanist Manifesto II is said to be "a positive declaration for times of uncertainty."

Assault on Christianity

Immediately, in the very next paragraph of the preface, a scathing attack on Christianty is launched. The idea of a "prayer-hearing God" is said to be "an unproved and outmoded faith." "Salvationism, based on mere affirmation, still appears as harmful, diverting people with false hopes of heaven hereafter. Reasonable minds look to other means for survival." It should be noted with care that this initial anti-God statement appears in the third paragraph of the preface, immediately following the claim that *Manifesto II* is "a positive declaration."

The introduction boldly proclaims that "the next century can be and should be the humanistic century." Traditional moral codes are no longer adequate. Belief is needed in the possibilities of human progress. The "set of common principles" contained in this manifesto represents "a design for a secular society on a planetary scale." This new *Humanist Manifesto* is presented "for the future of mankind" as "a vision of hope."

Self-Salvation and "Rights"

Understandably, *Religion* is the first of the six major topics discussed. ". . . traditional dogmatic or authoritarian religions that place revelation, God, ritual, or creed above human needs and experience do a disservice to the human species." The authors flatly declare, " . . . we find insufficient evidence for belief in the existence of a supernatural; it is either meaningless or irrelevant to the question of the survival and fulfillment of the human race. As nontheists, we begin with humans not God, nature not deity . . . . "

The humanist program to rule God out of the affairs of men is brought into sharp focus in the final sentence of the very first section with the statement, "No deity will save us: we must save ourselves." The second section states that promises of "immortal salvation or fear of eternal damnation" are both "illusory and harmful." Man has emerged from "natural evolutionary forces," and there is "no credible evidence that life survives the death of the body."

The third and fourth sections of the *Manifesto* fall under the general heading of *Ethics*. According to Point Three, " . . . moral values derive their source from human experience. Ethics is *autonomous* and *situational*, needing no theological or ideological sanction." The fourth section calls for the application of "reason and intelligence" and "the controlled use of scientific method" for the solution of human problems.

The fifth and sixth sections relate to the individual. " . . . We reject all religious, ideological, or moral codes that denigrate the individual, suppress freedom, dull intellect, dehumanize personality." Section six decries "intolerant attitudes" toward sexuality, which are often cultivated by "orthodox religions and puritanical cultures." The right to "birth control, abortion, and divorce should be recognized."

National and World Problems

Sections 7 through 11 deal with democratic society, calling for "a full range of civil liberties," the right to die with dignity, euthanasia, and the right to suicide. The commitment to "an open and democratic society" is voiced, and the statement is made that "bureaucratic structures" should be held to a minimum. The separation of church and state is imperative. Economic systems should be evaluated on the basis of their ability to "increase the sum of human satisfaction, and enhance the quality of life." The "principle of moral equality" should be upheld in matters of race, religion, sex, age, and national origin. There should be adequate care for the unfortunate, and universal education should be provided for all.

Sections 12 through 17 are presented under the general heading *World Community*. Nationalism is to be deplored. A world community needs to be built, commensurate with the development of "a system of world law and world order based upon transnational federal government." Violence and force must be renounced as a method of solving international disputes. War is obsolete. International courts must be established for peaceful adjudication of differences. The resources of the earth must be conserved, and it is the obligation of the more developed nations to provide "massive technical, agricultural, medical, and economic assistance" to the less-developed portions of the world. "World poverty must cease." Communication and transportation across frontiers must be expanded, and travel restrictions must no longer be imposed.

Under a closing section entitled *Humanity as a Whole*, a ringing appeal is made for "commitment to all humankind" as "the highest commitment of which we are capable." We must move toward a "wider vision of human potentiality," with each person becoming "a citizen of a world community."

The unyielding optimism of *Manifesto II* is evident in its very last sentence: "We believe that humankind has the potential intelligence, good will, and cooperative skill to implement this commitment in the decades ahead."

Man in Rebellion

Christians will recognize *Humanist Manifesto II* as a pathetic document created by lost men tottering on the brink of eternity and whistling into the darkness of space. It is a document in which man has ruled his Creator out of existence. It asserts that man is good and God is bad. Accordingly, man has no source of

values, no ultimate point of reference, no high commitment, no hope except in himself. Man finds his reason
for being in the mere fact of his existence rather than
in the service of the God of the universe. Man expresses
his contempt for ultimate reality, for eternity, for life
beyond the doorway of death.

Humanism is man's effort to eliminate God from
his thinking and to live as if God did not exist. It is
man attempting to solve his problems apart from God.
It is man in league with Satan and in rebellion against
the authority of the Most High. It is man's effort to
construct his own heaven on earth, without the help of
our Lord and Savior, Jesus Christ.

A few appropriate words from God, selected from
chapter 38 of Job, are appropriate for all humanists:

> "Where were you when I laid the foundation
> of the earth! Have you ever in your life com-
> manded the morning, And caused the dawn to
> know its place; Have you entered into the springs
> of the sea? Or have you walked in the recesses of
> the deep? Who has cleft a channel for the flood,
> or a way for the thunderbolt; Can you bind the
> chains of the Pleiades, or loose the cords of Orion?
> Do you know the ordinances of the heavens, or
> fix their rule over the earth?"

Christians and Humanism

It is highly important for Christians everywhere
to recognize the nature and intent of the rising

humanist movement. More and more it is necessary for the discerning Christian to apply the following acid test to all ideologies and to the policies and platforms of new groups which appear on the scene: "Is it of God, or is it of man?" The same test should be applied when humanism manifests itself in the educational system, in the world of politics, in economics, literature, art, entertainment, foreign policy, business, philosophy, religion, and elsewhere.

The only adequate answer to humanism is true Christianity, expressed consistently in all areas of life. Bible study *is* important—but it isn't enough. Attending church *is* important—but it isn't enough. Personal soul-winning is also very important—but it isn't sufficient to stem the tide of Godless humanism, which has already taken control of our schools, our courts, our economy, our government, and many of our churches. If Christianity-as-usual could turn back the oncoming tide of humanist influence, it would already have done so.

What is needed in this hour is a living dynamic faith in Jesus Christ and His Resurrection power—a faith which will produce a great new emphasis on Christianity-in-action. Christians must become very practical. We must study the Bible with a purpose. We must study the Bible to discover the great principles which provide guidance and direction for the people of God today. We must formulate programs based on the Word of God and move into action with these programs—in education, business, law, morals, communications, public leadership, and government.

The moving force behind humanism is Satan. Humanism is basically Satan's philosophy and program. Certain features of it may sound reasonable, but it always leads to tragedy, simply because it ignores the guidance of God. Only our Christian citizens have the discernment to evaluate humanism for what it is. Therefore our Christian citizens represent the only force capable of defeating it.

Confrontation and Constructiveness

However, we Christians must be realistic. We must realize that we cannot simply "wish" the devil's age-long program away. We must do battle openly against it. We must engage in an open confrontation with evil in all areas of life. Christians everywhere must believe the Word of God and follow up with the action which that belief produces. Do you doubt that this is practical?

What use is it, my brethren, if a man says he has faith, but he has no works? Can that faith save him? If a brother or sister is without clothing and in need of daily food, and one of you says to them, "Go in peace, be warmed and be filled," and yet you do not give them what is necessary for their body, what use is that? Even so faith, if it has not works, is dead, being by itself.

James 2:14–17

What is your faith producing these days? Are you trusting God to enable you to change things you do not like? Is is happening? You see, your faith is dead and useless if it accomplishes nothing. Christianity must be practical and effectual against the mounting turbulance of our age or it is worthless. We must look to God for energy to set forth on a campaign of advancing the application of God's Word both locally and nationally.

Christians of all denominations must openly fight for righteousness whenever and wherever humanism in any form raises its evil head. We must develop constructive, biblically based programs designed to deal effectively with the whole range of problems and issues which afflict us today. These programs must be rooted in eternal truth so as to assure their effectiveness. And they must reflect glory and praise to Almighty God, the Creator of all things.

Put on the full armor of God, that you may be able to stand firm against the schemes of the devil. For our struggle is not against flesh and blood, but against the rulers, against the powers, against the world forces of this darkness, against the spiritual forces of wickedness in the heavenly places. Therefore, take up the full armor of God, that you may be able to resist in the evil day, and having done everything, to stand firm.

Ephesians 6:11–13

Note: Appendix A features an analytical exposure of Humanist ideology in comparison with biblical teachings. Appendix B presents the full unedited text of *Humanist Manifesto I*, followed by the names of its signers. Appendix C features the full text of *Humanist Manifesto II*, together with the names of its signers. These "manifestos" are included for the convenience of readers who will want to use them for reference and study purposes.

APPENDIX A
The Teachings
of Humanism

ANALYSIS

Traditional Belief System of the Bible	Comprehensive Belief System of Humanism
God, creation, morality, the fallen state of man, redemption through Christ and the free-enterprise capitalist system.	Rejection of God and substitution of evolution, amorality, basic goodness of man, and one-world socialist system.
God has written His values (the Bible) and if man obeys he will be prosperous and have life (love, joy, peace, patience, gentleness, kindness, dependability, goodness and self-control).	Man is to follow his own changing values and society must be responsible for the consequences of his actions (abortion, illegitimate births, lesbianism, homosexuality, murder, hatred, strife).

Biblical System	Humanist System
God has made man in His image—spirit, soul and body—to be in fellowship with Him.	Man is an animal (soul and body) and needs only to be in fellowship with himself.
God is Supreme Being, therefore faith and trust are in Him.	Man is Supreme Being, therefore faith and trust is in man.
God does not change (there is certainty) therefore this system includes law which defines certainty.	There is *no certainty* because there is constant change (evolution); therefore law must be continually changed.
God is a supernatural being, omnipotent (all powerful), omnipresent (present everywhere), omniscient (knowledge of everything).	Humanism teaches *psychic phenomena* to give man (supreme being) the sense (feeling) of being supernatural. Psycho trip.
We have to answer directly to God for our actions ultimately.	Humanism teaches— the individual need answer only to himself.
Life after Death.	No life after death.
Lying is wrong, regardless what the liar thinks.	Lying doesn't exist if the liar thinks it is OK.
There is a devil (Satan).	There is no devil.

Biblical System	Humanist System
God's name should not be profaned, because God should be respected above all.	Humanism allows the profaning of God's name since God does not exist.
Man is basically evil, separated from God and God has to determine a set of values for him.	Humanism teaches— Man is basically good and therefore is able to determine his own values by himself.
The law is the authority that establishes the boundary of conduct.	No man need recognize any authority beyond himself.
God has freely given, (by grace) Jesus Christ (so that man can be reconciled to God).	Humanism teaches— there is no sin and man needs to be reconciled *only* to himself.
Man is able to freely receive the benefits of God's grace by faith.	Man's faith is in himself and he must create his own benefits.
Men and women are different.	Men and women are the same.
The family is the basic unit of society. The family is responsible to fulfill physical necessities.	The individual is the basic unit of society. Society is responsible to fulfill physical necessities.

Biblical System	Humanist System
God is love.	Sex is love.
Do unto others as you would have them do unto you. (Forgiveness is required here).	Humanism teaches— love is never having to say "I'm sorry". (No need for forgiveness).
Sex is for procreation and we are to multiply and inhabit the land.	We are overpopulated (a lie) and must stop having babies.
Sex is a beautiful relationship between husband and wife who have become one flesh.	Sex is a physical animal need that must be gratified in any way that the person craves.
The sovereignty of each nation to govern itself.	One-world system ruled by an intellectual elite.
There are absolute rights and wrongs.	There are *no* absolute rights and wrongs.
Guilt and shame result when a person does something wrong (sin) according to that which is written (the law of God).	No guilt and shame exist because no one can do any wrong (sin). Wrong (sin) does not exist, therefore guilt and shame do not exist.
Certain absolute moral values.	Uncertain, amoral values.

Biblical System	Humanist System
Prostitution, incest and abortion-on-demand are wrong.	Prostitution, incest and abortion-on-demand are OK.
Homosexuality (sodomy) is wrong.	Homosexuality (sodomy) is OK.
Lesbianism is wrong.	Lesbianism is OK.
Sex outside marriage (fornication, adultery, etc.) is wrong.	Sex outside marriage (fornication, adultery, etc.) is OK.
Public nudity is wrong.	Public nudity is OK.
Sensuality and sexual activities should be in private.	Sensuality and sexual activities in public are acceptable conduct.
Pornography is wrong.	Pornography is OK.
Use of drugs is wrong.	Use of drugs is OK.
Suicide is wrong.	Suicide is OK.
Killing of old people and sick persons (euthanasia) is wrong.	Killing of old people and sick persons (euthanasia) is OK.

Humanism, Feminism, & Marxism

In *Humanist Magazine* (November/December 1980) author Riane Eisler, author of *The Equal Rights Handbook*, says: "It is absurd to say . . . that one is a humanist but not a feminist . . . feminism is the last evolutionary development of humanism. Feminism is humanism on its most advanced level"

Karl Marx's own definition of Humanism reads: "Humanism is the denial of God, and the total affirmation of man . . . . Humanism is really nothing else but Marxism." (Karl Marx, Economic Politique et Philosophie, Vol. 1, pages 38–40).

"Soviet society today is the real embodiment of the ideas of proletarian, socialist humanism." (*On The Policy of The Soviet Union and The International Situation*, by Leonid Brezhnev, prepared by the Novosti Press Agency Publishing House, Moscow—Doubleday & Company, Inc., Garden City, N.Y., 1973, page 27).

"Soviet society today is the real embodiment of the ideas of proletarian, socialist humanism." (*On The Policy of The Soviet Union and The International Situation*, by Leonid Brezhnev, prepared by the Novosti Press Agency Publishing House, Moscow—Doubleday & Company, Inc., Garden City, N.Y., 1973, page 27).

APPENDIX B
Humanist
Manifesto I
(1933)

FULL TEXT, UNEDITED

The time has come for widespread recognition of the radical changes in religious beliefs throughout the modern world. The time is past for mere revision of traditional attitudes. Science and economic change have disrupted the old beliefs. Religions the world over are under the necessity of coming to terms with new conditions created by a vastly increased knowledge and experience. In every field of human activity, the vital movement is now in the direction of a candid and explicit humanism. In order that religious humanism may be better understood we, the undersigned, desire to make certain affirmations which we believe the facts of our contemporary life demonstrate.

There is great danger of a final, and we believe fatal, identification of the word *religion* with doctrines and methods which have lost their significance and which are powerless to solve the problem of human living in the Twentieth Century. Religions have always been means for realizing the highest values of life. Their end has been accomplished through the interpretation of the total environing situation (theology for world view), the sense of values resulting thereform (goal or ideal), and the technique (cult) established for realizing the satisfactory life. A change in any of these factors rsults in alteration of the outward forms of religion. This fact explains the changefulness of religions through the centuries. But through all changes religion itself remains constant in its quest for abiding values, an inseparable feature of human life.

Today man's larger understanding of the universe, his scientific achievements, and his deeper appreciation of brotherhood, have created a situation which requires a new statement of the means and purposes of religion. Such a vital, fearless, and frank religion capable of furnishing adequate social goals and personal satisfactions may appear to many people as a complete break with the past. While this age does owe a vast debt to traditional religions, it is none the less obvious that any religion that can hope to be a synthesizing and dynamic force for today must be shaped for the needs of this age. To establish such a religion is a major necessity of the present. It is a responsibility which rests upon this generation. We thereform affirm the following:

First: Religious humanists regard the universe as self-existing and not created.

Second: Humanism believes that man is a part of nature and that he has emerged as the result of a continuous process.

Third: Holding an organic view of life, humanists find that the traditional dualism of mind and body must be rejected.

Fourth: Humanism recognizes that man's religious culture and civilization, as clearly depicted by anthropology and history, are the product of a gradual development due to his interaction with his natural environment and with his social heritage. The individual born into a particular culture is largely molded to that culture.

Fifth: Humanism asserts that the nature of the universe depicted by modern science makes unacceptable any supernatural or cosmic guarantees of human values. Obviously humanism does not deny the possibility of realities as yet undiscovered, but it does insist that the way to determine the existence and value of any and all realities is by means of intelligent inquiry and by the assessment of their relation to human needs. Religion must formulate its hopes and plans in the light of the scientific spirit and method.

Sixth: We are convinced that the time has passed for theism, deism, modernism, and the several varieties of "new thought."

Seventh: Religion consists of those actions, purposes, and experiences which are humanly significant. Nothing human is alien to the religious. It includes labor, art, science, philosophy, love, friendship, recreation—all that is in its degree expressive of intelligently satisfying human living. The distinction between the sacred and the secular can no longer be maintained.

Eighth: Religious humanism considers the complete realization of human personality to be the end of man's life and seeks its development and fulfillment in the here and now. This is the explanation of the humanist's social passion.

Ninth: In place of the old attitudes involved in worship and prayer the humanist finds his religious emotions expressed in a heightened sense of personal life and in a cooperative effort to promote social well-being.

Tenth: It follows that there will be no uniquely religious emotions and attitudes of the kind hitherto associated with belief in the supernatural.

Eleventh: Man will learn to face the crises of life in terms of his knowledge of their naturalness and probability. Reasonable and manly attitudes will be fostered by education and supported by custom. We assume that humanism will take the path of social and mental hygiene and discourage sentimental and unreal hopes and wishful thinking.

Twelth: Believing that religion must work increasingly for joy in living, religious humanists aim to foster the creative in man and to encourage achievements that add to the satisfactions of life.

Thirteenth: Religious humanism maintains that all

associations and institutions exist for the fulfillment of human life. The intelligent evaluation, transformation, control, and direction of such associations and institutions with a view to the enhancement of human life is the purpose and program of humanism. Certainly religious institutions, their ritualistic forms, ecclesiastical methods, and communal activities must be reconstituted as rapidly as experience allows, in order to function effectively in the modern world.

Fourteenth: The humanists are firmly convinced that existing acquisitive and profit-motivated society has shown itself to be inadequate and that a radical change in methods, controls, and motives must be instituted. A socialized and cooperative economic order must be established to the end that the equitable distribution of the means of life be possible. The goal of humanism is a free and universal society in which people voluntarily and intelligently cooperate for the common good. Humanists demand a shared life in a shared world.

Fifteenth and last: We assert that humanism will: (a) affirm life rather than deny it; (b) seek to elicit the possibilities of life, not flee from it; and (c) endeavor to establish the conditions of a satisfactory life for all, not merely for the few. By this positive morale and intention humanism will be guided, and from this perspective and alignment the techniques and efforts of humanism will flow.

So stand the theses of religious humanism. Though

we consider the religious forms and ideas of our fathers
no longer adequate, the quest for the good life is still
the central task for mankind. Man is at last becoming
aware that he alone is responsible for the realization
of the world of his dreams, that he has within himself
the power for its achievement. He must set intelligence
and will to the task.

J. A. C. Fagginer Auer

E. Burdette Backus

Harry Elmer Barnes

L. M. Birkhead

Raymond B. Bragg

Edwin Arthur Burtt

Ernest Caldecott

A. J. Carlson

John Dewey

Albert C. Dieffenbach

John H. Dietrich

Bernard Fantus

William Floyd

F. H. Hankins

A. Eustace Haydon

Llewellyn Jones

Robert Morss Lovett

Harold P. Marley

R. Lester Mondale

Charles Francis Potter

John Herman Randall, Jr.

Curtis W. Reese

APPENDIX C
Humanist
Manifesto II
(1973)

FULL TEXT, UNEDITED

Preface

It is forty years since Humanist Manifesto I (1933) appeared. Events since then make that earlier statement far too optimistic. Nazism has shown the depths of brutality of which humanity is capable. Other totalitarian regimes have suppressed human rights without ending poverty. Science has sometimes brought evil as well as good. Recent decades have shown that inhuman wars can be made in the name of peace. The beginnings of police states, even in democratic societies, widespread government espionage, and other abuses of power by military, political and industrial elites, and the continuance of unyielding racism, all present a different and difficult social outlook. In various societies, the demands of women and minority groups for equal rights effectively challenge our generation.

As we approach the twenty-first century, however, an affirmative and hopeful vision is needed. Faith, commensurate with advancing knowledge, is also necessary. In the choice between despair and hope, humanists respond in this Humanist Manifesto II with a positive declaration for times of uncertainty.

As in 1933, humanists still believe that traditional theism, especially faith in the prayer-hearing God, assumed to love and care for persons, to hear and understand their prayers and to be able to do something about them, is an unproven and outmoded faith. Salvationism based on mere affirmation, still appears as harmful, diverting people with false hopes of heaven hereafter. Reasonable minds look to other means for survival.

Those who sign Humanist Manifesto II disclaim that they are setting forth a binding credo; their individual views would be stated in widely varying ways. This statement is, however, reaching for vision in a time that needs direction. It is social analysis in an effort at consensus. New statements should be developed to supercede this, but for today it is our conviction that humanism offers an alternative that can serve present-day needs and guide humankind toward the future.

PAUL KURTS, *Editor*
EDWIN H. WILSON, *Editor Emeritus*

THE HUMANIST

Humanist Manifesto II

The next century can be and should be the humanistic century. Dramatic scientific, technological, and ever-accelerating social and political changes crowd our awareness. We have virtually conquered the planet, explored the moon, overcome the natural limits of travel and communication: we stand at the dawn of a new age; ready to move farther into space and perhaps inhabit other planets. Using technology wisely, we can control our environment, conquer poverty, markedly reduce disease, extend our lifespan, significantly modify our behavior, alter the course of human evolution and cultural development, unlock vast new powers, and provide humankind with unparalleled opportunity for achieving an abundant and meaningful life.

The future is, however, filled with dangers. In learning to apply the scientific method to nature and human life, we have opened the door to ecological damage, overpopulation, dehumanizing institutions, totalitarian repression, and nuclear and biochemical disaster. Faced with apocalyptic prophesies and doomsday scenarios, many flee in despair from reason and embrace irrational cults and theologies of withdrawal and retreat.

Traditional moral codes and newer irrational cults both fail to meet the pressing needs of today and tomorrow. False "theologies of hope" and messianic ideologies, substituting new dogmas for old, cannot cope with existing world realities. They separate rather than unite peoples.

Humanity, to survive, requires bold and daring measures. We need to extend the uses of scientific method, not renounce them, to fuse reason with compassion in order to build constructive social and moral values.

Confronted by many possible futures, we must decide which to pursue. The ultimate goal should be the fulfillment of the potential for growth in each human personality—not for the favored few, but for all of humankind. Only a shared world and global measures will suffice.

A humanist outlook will tap the creativity of each human being and provide the vision and courage for us to work together. This outlook emphasizes the role human beings can play in their own spheres of action. The decades ahead call for dedicated, clear-minded men and women able to marshal the will, intelligence, and cooperative skills for shaping a desirable future. Humanism can provide the purpose and inspiration that so many seek; it can give personal meaning and significance to human life.

Many kinds of humanism exist in the contemporary world. The varieties and emphases of naturalistic humanism include "scientific," "ethical," "democratic," "religious," and "Marxist" humanism. Free thought, atheism, agnosticism, skepticism, deism, rationalism, ethical culture, and liberal religion all claim to be heir to the humanist tradition. Humanism traces its roots from ancient China, classical Greece and Rome, through the Renaissance and the Enlightenment, to the scientific revolution of the modern world. But views that merely reject theism are not equivalent to humanism. They lack commitment to the positive belief in the possibilities of human progress and to the values central to it. Many within religious groups, believing in the future of humanism, now claim humanist credentials. Humanism is an ethical process through which we all can move, above and beyond the divisive particulars, heroic personalities, dogmatic creeds, and ritual customs of past religions or their mere negation.

We affirm a set of common principles that can serve as a basis for united action—positive principles relevant to the present human condition. They are a design for a secular society on a planetary scale.

For these reasons, we submit this new *Humanist Manifesto* for the future of humankind; for us, it is a vision of hope, a direction for satisfying survival.

Religion

First: In the best sense, religion may inspire dedication to the highest ethical ideals. The cultivation of moral devotion and creative imagination is an expression of genuine "spiritual" experience and aspiration.

We believe, however, that traditional dogmatic or authoritarian religions that place revelation, God, ritual, or creed above human needs and experience do a disservice to the human species. Any account of nature should pass the tests of scientific evidence; in our judgment, the dogmas and myths of traditional religions do not do so. Even at this late date in human history, certain elementary facts based upon the critical use of scientific reason have to be restated. *We find insufficient evidence for belief in the existence of a super-natural;* it is either meaningless or irrelevant to the question of the survival and fulfillment of the human race. *As non-theists, we begin with humans not God, nature not deity.* Nature may indeed be broader and deeper than we now know; any new discoveries, however, will but enlarge our knowledge of the natural.

Some humanists believe we should reinterpret traditional religions and reinvest them with meanings appropriate to the current situation. Such redefinitions, however, often perpetuate old dependencies and escapisms; they easily become obscurantist, impeding the free use of the intellect. We need, instead, radically new human purposes and goals.

We appreciate the need to preserve the best ethical teachings in the religious traditions of humankind, many of which we share in common. But *we reject those features of traditional religious morality that deny humans a full appreciation of their own potentialities and responsibilities. Traditional religions often offer solace to humans,* but, as often, they *inhibit humans from helping themselves* or experiencing their full potentials. Such institutions, creeds, and rituals often impede the will to serve others.

Too often traditional faiths encourage dependence rather that independence, obedience rather than affirmation, fear rather than courage. More recently they have generated concerned social action, with many signs of relevance appearing in the wake of the "God Is Dead" theologies. *But we can discover no divine purpose or providence for the human species.* While there is much that we do not know, *humans are responsible for what we are or will become. No deity will save us; we must save ourselves.*

Second: Promises of immortal salvation or fear of eternal damnation are both illusory and harmful. They distract humans from present concerns, from self-actualization, and from rectifying social injustices. Modern science discredits such historic concepts as the "ghost in the machine" and the "separable soul." Rather, science affirms that the human species is an emergence from natural evolutionary forces. As far as we know, the total personality is a function of the biological organism transacting in a social and cultural context. There is no credible evidence that life survives the death of the body. We continue to exist in our progeny and in the way that our lives have influenced others in our culture.

Traditional religions are surely not the only obstacles to human progress. Other ideologies also impede human advance. Some forms of political doctrine, for instance, function religiously, reflecting the worst features of orthodoxy and authoritarianism, especially when they sacrifice individuals on the altar of Utopian promises. Purely economic and political viewpoints, whether capitalist or communist, often function as religious and ideological dogma. Although humans undoubtedly need economic and political goals, they also need creative values by which to live.

Ethics

Third: We affirm that moral values derive their source from human experience. Ethics is autonomous and situational, needing no theological or ideological sanction. Ethics stems from human need and interest. To deny this distorts the whole basis of life. Human life has meaning because we create and develop our futures. Happiness and the creative realization of human needs and desires, individually and in shared enjoyment, are continuous themes of humanism. We strive for the good life, here and now. The goal is to pursue life's enrichment despite debasing forces of vulgarization, commercialization, bureaucratization, and dehumanization.

Fourth: Reason and intelligence are the most effective instruments that humankind possesses. There is no substitute; neither faith nor passion suffices in itself. The controlled use of scientific methods, which have transformed the natural and social sciences since the Renaissance, must be extended further in the solution of human problems. But reason must be tempered by humility, since no group has a monopoly on wisdom or virtue. Nor is there any guarantee that all problems can be solved or all questions answered. Yet critical intelligence, infused by a sense of human caring, is the best method that humanity has for resolving problems. Reason should be balanced with compassion and empathy and the whole person fulfilled. Thus, we are not advocating the use of scientific intelligence independent of or in opposition to emotion, for we believe in the cultivation of feeling and love. As science pushes back the boundary of the known, man's sense of wonder is continually renewed, and art, poetry, and music find their places, along with religion and ethics.

The Individual

Fifth: The preciousness and dignity of the individual person is a central humanist value. Individuals should be encouraged to realize their own creative talents and desires. We reject all religious, ideological, or moral codes that denigrate the individual, suppress freedom, dull intellect, dehumanize personality. We believe in maximum individual autonomy consonant with social responsibility. Although science can account for the causes of behavior, the possibilities of individual freedom of choice exist in human life and should be increased.

Sixth: In the area of sexuality, we believe that intolerant attitudes, often cultivated by orthodox religions and puritanical cultures, unduly repress sexual conduct. The right to birth control, abortion, and divorce should be recognized. While we do not approve of exploitive, denigrating forms of sexual expression, neither do we wish to prohibit, by law or social sanction, sexual behavior between consenting adults. The many varieties of sexual exploration should not in themselves by considered "evil." Without countenancing mindless permissiveness or unbridled promiscuity, a civilized society should be a tolerant one. Short of harming others or compelling them to do likewise, individuals should be permitted to express their sexual proclivities and pursue their life-styles as they desire. We wish to cultivate the development of a responsible attitude toward sexuality, in which humans are not exploited as sexual objects, and in which intimacy, sensitivity, respect, and honesty in interpersonal relations are encouraged. Moral education for children and adults is an important way of developing awareness and sexual maturity.

Democratic Society

Seventh: To enhance freedom and dignity the individual must experience a full range of *civil liberties* in all societies. This includes freedom of speech and the press, political democracy, the legal right of opposition to governmental policies, fair judicial process, religious liberty, freedom of association, and artistic, scientific, and cultural freedom. It also includes a recognition of an individual's right to die with dignity, euthanasia, and the right to suicide. We oppose the increasing invasion of privacy, by whatever means, in both totalitarian and democratic societies. We would safeguard, extend, and implement the principles of human freedom evolved from the *Magna Carta* to the *Bill of Rights,* the *Rights of Man,* and the *Universal Declaration of Human Rights.*

Eighth: We are committed to an open and democratic society. We must extend participatory democracy in its true sense to the economy, the school, the family, the workplace, and voluntary associations. Decision-making must be decentralized to include widespread involvement of people at all levels—social, political, and economic. All persons should have a voice in developing the values and goals that determine their lives. Institutions should be responsive to expressed desires and needs. The conditions of work, education, devotion, and play should be humanized. Alienating forces should be modified or eradicated and bureaucratic structures should be held to a minimum. People are more important than decalogues, rules, proscriptions, or regulations.

Ninth: The separation of church and state and the separation of ideology and state are imperatives. The state should encourage maximum freedom for different moral, political, religious, and social values in society. It should not favor any particular religious bodies through the use of public monies, nor espouse a single ideology and function thereby as an instrument of propaganda or oppression, particularly against dissenters.

Tenth: Humane societies should evaluate economic systems not by rhetoric or ideology, but by whether or not they increase economic well-being for all individuals and groups, minimize poverty and hardship, increase the sum of human satisfaction, and enhance the quality of life. Hence the door is open to alternative economic systems. We need to democratize the economy and judge it by its responsiveness to human needs, testing results in terms of the common good.

Eleventh: The principle of moral equality must be furthered through elimination of all discrimination based upon race, religion, sex, age, or national origin. This means equality of opportunity and recognition of talent and merit. Individuals should be encouraged to contribute to their own betterment. If unable, then society should provide means to satisfy their basic economic, health, and cultural needs, including, wherever resources make possible, a minimum guaranteed annual income. We are concerned for the welfare of the aged, the infirm, the disadvantaged, and also for the outcasts—the mentally retarded, abandoned, or abused children, the handicapped, prisoners, and addicts—for *all* who are neglected or ignored by society. Practicing humanists should make it their vocation to humanize personal relations.

We believe in the *right to universal education*. Everyone has a right to the cultural opportunity to fulfill his or her unique capacities and talents. The schools should foster satisfying and productive living. They should be open at all levels to any and all, the achievement of excellence should be encouraged. Innovative and experimental forms of education are to be welcomed. The energy and idealism of the young deserve to be appreciated and channeled to constructive purposes.

We deplore racial, religious, ethnic, or class antagonisms. Although we believe in cultural diversity and encourage racial and ethnic pride, we reject separations which promote alienation and set people and groups against each other; we envision an *integrated* community where people have a maximum opportunity for free and voluntary association.

We are *critical of sexism or sexual chauvinism*—male or female. We believe in equal rights for both women and men to fulfill their unique careers and potentialities as they see fit, free of invidious discrimination.

World Community

Twelfth: We deplore the division of humankind on nationalistic grounds. We have reached a turning point in human history where the best option is to *transcend the limits of national sovereignty* and to move toward the building of a world community in which all sectors of the human family can participate. Thus we look to the development of a system of world law and a world order based upon transnational federal government. This would appreciate cultural pluralism and diversity. It would not exclude pride in national origins and accomplishments nor the handling of regional problems on a regional basis. Human progress, however, can no longer be achieved by focusing on one section of the world. Western or Eastern, developed or undeveloped, for the first time in human history, no part of humankind can be isolated from any other. Each person's future is in some way linked to all. We thus reaffirm a commitment to the building of world community, at the same time recognizing that this commits us to some hard choices.

Thirteenth: This world community must *renounce the resort to violence and force* as a method of solving international disputes. We believe in the peaceful adjudication of differences by international courts and by the development of the arts of negotiation and compromise. War is obsolete. So is the use of nuclear, biological, and chemical weapons. It is a planetary imperative to reduce the level of military expenditures and turn these savings to peaceful and people-oriented uses.

Fourteenth: *The world community must engage in cooperative planning* concerning the use of rapidly depleting resources. The planet earth must be considered a single *ecosystem*. Ecological damage, resource depletion, and excessive population growth must be checked by international concord. The cultivation and conservation of nature is a moral value; we should perceive ourselves as integral to the sources of our being in nature. We must free our world from needless pollution and waste, responsibly guarding and creating wealth, both natural and human. Exploitation of natural resources, uncurbed by social conscience, must end.

Fifteenth: The problems of *economic growth and development* can no longer be resolved by one nation alone; they are worldwide in scope. It is the moral obligation of the developed nations to provide—through an international authority that safeguards human rights—massive technical, agricultural, medical, and economic assistance, including birth control techniques, to the developing portions of the globe. World poverty must cease. Hence extreme disproportions in wealth, income, and economic growth should be reduced on a worldwide basis.

Sixteenth: Technology is a vital key to human progress and development. We deplore any neo-romantic efforts to condemn indiscriminately all technology and science or to counsel retreat from its further extension and use for the good of humankind. We would resist any moves to censor basic scientific research on moral, political, or social grounds. Technology must, however, be carefully judged by the consequences of its use; harmful and destructive changes should be avoided. We are particularly disturbed when technology and bureaucracy control, manipulate, or modify human beings without their consent. Technological feasibility does not imply social or cultural desirability.

Seventeenth: We must expand communication and transportation across frontiers. Travel restrictions must cease. The world must be open to diverse political, ideological, and moral viewpoints and evolve a worldwide system of television and radio for information and education. We thus call for full international cooperation in culture, science, the arts, and technology *across ideological borders*. We must learn to live openly together or we shall all perish together.

Humanity as a Whole

In closing: The world cannot wait for a reconciliation of competing political or economic systems to solve its problems. These are the times for men and women of good will to further the building of a peaceful and prosperous world. We urge that parochial loyalties and inflexible moral and religious ideologies be transcended. We urge recognition of the common humanity of all people. We further urge the use of reason and compassion to produce the kind of world we want—a world in which peace, prosperity, freedom, and happiness are widely shared. Let us not abandon that vision in despair or cowardice. We are responsible for what we are or will be. Let us work together for a humane world by means commensurate with humane ends. Destructive ideological differences among communism, capitalism, socialism, conservatism, liberalism, and radicalism should be overcome. Let us call for an end to terror and hatred. We will survive and prosper in a world of shared humane values. We can initiate new directions for humankind; ancient rivalries can be superseded by broad-based cooperative efforts. The commitment to tolerance, understanding, and peaceful negotiation does not necessitate acquiescence to the status quo or the damming up of dynamic and revolutionary forces. The true revolution is occurring and can continue in countless non-violent adjustments. But this entails the willingness to step forward into new and expanding plateaus. At the present juncture of history, commitment to all humankind is the highest commitment to which we are capable; it transcends the narrow allegiances of church, state, party, class, or race in moving toward a wider version of human potentiality. What more daring goal for humankind than for each person to become, in ideal as well as practice, a citizen of a world community. It is a classical vision; we can now give it new vitality. Humanism thus interpreted is a moral force that has time on its side. We believe that humankind has the potential intelligence, good will, and cooperative skill to implement this commitment in the decades ahead.

We, the undersigned, while not necessarily endorsing every detail of the above, plegde our general support to Humanist Manifesto II for the future of humankind.

These affirmations are not a final credo or dogma but an expression of a living and growing faith. We invite others in all lands to join us in further developing and working for these goals.

Signers

Lionel Abel, *Prof. of English, State Univ. of New York at Buffalo*

Khoren Arisian, *Board of Leaders, NY Soc. for Ethical Culture*

Isaac Asimov, *author*

George Axtelle, *Prof. Emeritus, Southern Illinois Univ.*

Archie J. Bahm, *Prof. of Philosophy Emeritus, Univ. of N.M.*

Paul H. Beattie, *Pres., Fellowship of Religious Humanists*

Keith Heggs, *Exec. Dir., American Humanist Association*

Malcolm Bissell, *Prof. Emeritus, University of Southern California*

H. J. Blackham, *Chm., Social Morality Council, Great Britain*

Brand Blanshard, *Prof. Emeritus, Yale Univ.*

Paul Blanshard, *author*

Joseph L. Blau, *Prof. of Religion, Columbia Univ.*

Sir Hermann Bondi, *Prof. of Math., King's Coll, Univ. of London*

Howard Box, *Leader, Brooklyn Soc. for Ethical Culture*

Raymond B. Bragg, *Minister Emeritus, Unitarian Ch., Kansas City*

Theodore Brameld, *Visiting Prof., C.U.N.Y.*
Brigid Brophy, *author, Great Britain*
Lester R. Brown, *Senior Fellow, Overseas Development Council*
Bette Chambers, *Pres., American Humanist Association*
John Ciardi, *poet*
Francis Crick, *M. D., Great Britain*
Arthur Danto, *Prof. of Philosophy, Columbia Univ.*
Lucien de Coninck, *Prof., University of Gund., Belgium*
Miriam Allen deFord, *author*
Edd Doerr, *Americans United for Separation of Church and State*
Peter Draper, *M. D., Guy's Hospital Medical School, London*
Paul Edwards, *Prof. of Philosophy, Brooklyn College*
Albert Ellis, *Exec. Dir., Inst. Adv. Study Rational Psychotherapy*
Edward L. Ericson, *Board of Leaders, NY Soc. for Ethical Culture*
H. J. Eysenck, *Prof. of Psychology, Univ. of London*
Roy P. Fairfield, *Coordinator, Union Graduate School*
Herbert Feigl, *Prof. Emeritus, Univ. of Minnesota*
Raymond Firth, *Prof. Emeritus of Anthropology, Univ. of London*
Anthony Flew, *Prof. of Philosophy, The Univ., Reading, England*
Kenneth Furness, *Exec. Secy., British Humanist Association*
Erwin Gaede, *Minister, Unitarian Church, Ann Arbor, Mich.*

Richard S. Gilbert, *Minister, First Unitarian Ch., Rochester, N.Y.*

Charles Wesley Grady, *Minister, First Unitarian Ch., Arlington, Ma.*

Maxine Greene, *Teachers College, Columbia Univ.*

Thomas C. Greening, *Editor,* Journal of Humanistic Psychology

Alan F. Guttmacher, *Pres., Planned Parenthood Fed. of America*

J. Harold Hadley, *Minister, Unit. Univ. Ch., Pt. Washington, N. Y.*

Hector Hawton, *Editor, Question,* Great Britain

A. Eustace Haydon, *Prof. Emeritus of History of Religions*

James Hemming, *Psychologist, Great Britain*

Palmer A. Hilty, *Adm. Secy., Fellowship of Religious Humanist*

Hudson Hoagland, *Pres. Emeritus, Worcester Fdn. for Exper. Bio.*

Robert S. Hoagland, Editor, Religious Humanism

Sidney Hook, *Prof. Emeritus of Philosophy, New York Univ.*

James F. Hornbock, *Leader, Ethical Soc. of St. Louis*

James M. Hutchinson, *Minister Emeritus, First Unit. Ch., Cincinnati*

Mordecai M. Kaplan, Rabbi Fndr. of Jewish Reconstr. Movement

John C. Kidnergn, *Prof. of Social Work., Univ. of Minnesota*

Lester A. Kirkendall, *Prof. Emeritus, Oregan State Univ.*

Margaret Knight, *Univ. of Aberdeen, Scotland*

Jean Kotkin, *Exec. Secy., American Ethica Union*
Richard Kostelanets, *poet*
Paul Kurtz, *editor,* The Humanist
Lawrence Lader, *Chm., Natl. Assn. for Repeal of Abortion Laws*
Edward Lamb, *Pres., Lamb Communications, Inc.*
Corliss Lamont, *Chm., Natl. Emergency Civil Liberties Union*
Chauncey D. Leake, *Prof., Univ. of California, San Francisco*
Alfred McC. Lee, *Prof. Emeritus, Soc. Anthropology, C.U.N.Y.*
Elizabeth Briant lee, *author*
Christopher Macy, *Dir., Rationalist Press Assn., Great Britain*
Clorinda Margolis, *Jefferson Comm. Mental Health Cen., Phila.*
Joseph Margolis, *Prof. of Philosophy, Temple Univ.*
Harold P. Marley, *Ret. Unitarian Minister*
Floyd W. Matson, *Prof. of American Studies, Univ. of Hawaii*
Lester Mondale, *former Pres., Fellowship of Religious Humanists*
Lloyd Morain, *Pres., Illinois Gas Company*
Mary Morain, *Editorial BJ., Intl. Soc. for General Semantics*
Charles Morris, *Prof. Emeritus, Univ. of Florida*
Henry Morgentaler, *M. D., Past Pres., Humanist Assn. of Canada*
Mary Mothersill, *Prof. of Philosophy, Barnard College*

Jerome Nathanson, *Chem., Bd. of Leaders, NY Soc. Ethical Culture*

Billy Joe Nichols, *Minister, Richardson Unitarian Church, Texas*

Kai Nielsen, *Prof. of Philosophy, University of Calgary, Canada*

P. H. Nowell-Smith, *Prof. of Philosophy, York Univ., Canada*

Chaim Perelman, *Prof. of Philosophy, Univ. of Brussels, Belgium*

James W. Prescott, *Natl. Inst. of Child Health and Human Dev.*

Harold J. Quigley, *Leader, Ethical Humanist Society of Chicago*

Howard Radest, *Prof. of Philosophy, Ramapo College*

John Herman Randall, Jr. *Prof. Emeritus, Columbia Univ.*

Oliver L. Reiser, *Prof. Emeritus, Univ. of Pittsburgh*

Lord Ritchie-Calder, *formerly Univ. of Edinburgh, Scotland*

B. T. Rocca, Jr., *Consultant, Intl. Trade and Commodities*

Andrei D. Sakharov, *Academy of Sciences, Moscow, U.S.S.R.*

Sidney H. Scheuer, *Chm., Natl. Comm. for an Effective Congress*

Herbert W. Schneider, *Prof. Emeritus, Claremont Grad. School*

Clinton Lee Scott, *Universalist Minister, St. Petersburgh, Fla.*

Roy Wood Sellars, *Prof., Emeritus, University of Michigan*

Appendix C: Humanist Manifesto II (1973)

A. B. Shah, *Pres. Indian Secular Society*
B. F. Skinner, *Prof. of Psychology, Harvard Univ.*
Kenneth J. Smith, *Leader, Philadelphia Ethical Society*
Matthew Ies Spetter, *Chm., Dept. Ethics, Ethical Culture Schools*
Mark Starr, *Chm. Esperanto Info. Center*
Svetozar Stojanovic, *prof. Philosophy, Univ. Belgrade, Yogoslavia*
Harold Taylor, *Project Director, World University Student Project*
V. T. Thayer, *author*
Herbert A. Tonne, Ed. Board. Journal of Business Education
Jack Tourin, *Pres., American Ethical Union*
E. C. Vanerlaan, *lecturer*
J. P. van Praag, *Chem., Intl. Humanist and Ethical Union, Utrecht*
Maurice B. Visscher, *M. D., Prof. Emeritus, Univ. of Minnesota*
Goodwin Watson, *Assn. Coordinator, Union Graduate School*
Gerald Wendt, *author*
Henry N. Wieman, *Prof. Emeritus, Univ. of Chicago*
Sherwin Wine, *Rabbi, Soc. for Humanistic Judaism*
Edwin H. Wilson, *Ex. Dir. Emeritus, American Humanist Assn.*
Bertram D. Wolfe, *Hoover Institution*
Alexander S. Yesenin Volpin, *mathematician*
Marvin Zimmerman, *Prof. of Philosophy, State Univ. NY at Bib.*

BANGLADESH:

Abul Hasanat, Secretary, Bangladesh Humanist Society

CANADA:

J. Lloyd Brereton, *ed., Humanist in Canada*
Andrew Malleson, M.S., *psychiatrist*
Eleanor Wright Peirine, *author*
Bernard Porter, *Pres., Toronto Humanist Assn.*

FRANCE:

Pierre Lamarque
Jacques Monod, *Institut Pasteur*
Jean-Francois Revel, *journalist*

GERMANY (WEST):

Waltre Behrendt, *Vice Pres., European Parliament*
W. Bonness, *Pres., Bund Freirelgioser Gemeinden*
D. Bronder, *Bund Freirelgioser Gemeinden*

GREAT BRITAIN:

Sir Alfred Ayer, *Prof., Oxford*
Sir Julian Huxley, *former hd., UNESCO*

INDIA:

G. D. Parikh, *Indian Radical Humanist Assn.*
A. Solomon, coordinator, Indian Secular Society
V. M. Tarkunde, *Pres., All Indian Radical Humanist Assn.*

NIGERIA:

Ernest N. Ukpaby, *Dean, Univ. of Nigeria*

PHILIPPINES:

Gonzalo Quiogue, *Vice Pres., Humanist Assn. of the Philippines*

SOVIET UNION:

Zhores Medvedev, *scientist*

SWEDEN:

Gunnar Myrdal, *Prof. Univ. of Stockholm*

U. S. A.:

Gina Allen, *author*
John C. Anderson, *Humanist Counselor*
Peter O. Anderson, *Asst. Prof., Ohio State Univ.*
William F. Anderson, *Humanist Counselor*

John Anton, *Prof., Emory University*
Celia Baker
Ernest Baker, *Assoc. Prof., Univ. of the Pacific*
Marjorie S. Baker, Ph. D., *Pres., Humanist Community of San Francisco*
Henry S. Basayne, *Assoc. Exec. Officer, Assn. for Humanistic Psychology*
Mildred H. Blum, *Sec'y., American Ethical Union*
Robert O. Boothe, *Prof. Emer., Cal. Polytechnic*
Clement A. Bosch
Madeline L. Bosch
Bruni Boyd, *Vice Pres., American Ethical Union*
Nancy Brewer, *Humanist Counselor*
Charles Brownfield, *Asst. Prof., Queensborough Community College, CUNY*
Constantia Brownfield, *R. N.,*
Margaret Brown, *Assoc. Prof., Oneota State Univ. College*
Beulah L. Bullard, *Humanist Counselor*
Joseph Chuman, *Leader, Ethical Soc. of Essex Co.*
Gordon Clanton, *Asst. Prof., Trenton State College*
Daniel S. Collins, *Leader, Unitarian Fellowshp of Jonesboro, Ark.*
Wm. Creque, *Pres., Fellowship of Humanity, Oakland, Ca.*
M. Benjamin Dell, *Dir. Amer. Humanist Assn.*
James Durant IV, *Prof., Polk Comm. College, Winter Haven, Fla.*
Gerald A. Ehrenreich, *Assoc. Prof., University of Kansas School of Medicine*
Marie Erdmann, *Teacher, Campbell Elem. Sch.*

Appendix C: Humanist Manifesto II (1973)

Robert L. Erdmann, *Ph. D., IBM*
Hans S. Falck, *Disting. Prof., Menninger Fdn*
James Farmer, *Dir. Public Policy Training Inst.*
Ed Farrar
Joe Felmet, *Humanist Counselor*
Thomas Ferrick, *Leader, Ethical Soc. of Boston*
Norman Fleishman, *Exec. Vice Pres., Planned Parenthood World Population, Los Angeles*
Joseph Fletcher, *Visiting Prof., Sch. of Medicine, Univ. of Virginia*
Douglas Frazier, *Leader, American Ethical Union*
Betty Friedan, *Founder, N. O. W.*
Harry M. Geduold, *Prof., Indiana University*
Roland Gibson, *Pres., Art Fdn. of Potsdam, N. Y.*
Aron S. Gilmartin, *Minister, Mt. Diablo Unitarian Church, Walnut Creek, Ca.*
Annabelle Glasser, *Dir., Amer. Ethical Union*
Rebecca Goldblum, *Dir. Amer. Ethical Union*
Louis R. Gomberg, *Humanist Counselor*
Harold N. Gordon, *Vice Pres., Amer. Ethic al Univ.*
Sol Gordon, *Prof., Syracuse University*
Theresa Gould, *American Ethical Union*
Gregory O. Grant, *Captain, USAF*
Ronald Green, *Asst. Prof., New York Univ.*
LeRue Grim, *Secretary, Amer Humanist Assn.*
S. Spencer Grin, *Pub.,* Saturday Review/World
Josephine G. Gurgard, *Sec'y. Humanist Society of Greater Philadelphia*
Samuel J. Gurbarg

Lewis M. Gubrud, *Exec. Dir., Mediator Fellowship, Providence, R.I.*

Frank A. Hall, *Minister, Murray Univ. Church, Attleboro, Mass.*

Harold Hansen, *Pres., Space Coast Chapter, AHA*

Ethelbert Haskins, *Dir., Amer. Humanist Assn.*

Lester H. Hayes, *Public Relations Dir., American Income Life Insurance Co.*

Donald E. Henshaw, *Humanist Counselor*

Alex Hersahft, *Principal Scientist, Booz Allen Applied Research*

Ronald E. Hestand, *author and columnist*

Irving Louis Horowitz, *editor,* Society

Warren S. Hoskins, *Humanist Counselor*

Mark W. Huber, *Director, Amer. Ethical Union*

Harold J. Hutchison, *Humanist Counselor*

Arthur M. Jackson, *Exec. Dir., Humanist Comm.,San Jose; Treasurer, Amer. Humanist Assn.*

Linda R. Jackson, *Dir., Amer. Humanist Assn.*

Steven Jacobs, *former Pres., Amer. Ethical Union*

Thomas B. Johnson, Jr., *consulting psychologist*

Robert Edward Jones, *Exec. Dir., Joint Washington Office for Social Concern*

Marion Kahn, *Pres., Humanist Society of Metropolitan New York*

Alec E. Kelley, *Prof., Univ. of Arizona*

Marvin Kohl, *Prof., SUNY at Fredonia*

RECOMMENDED FOR FURTHER READING AND LISTENING

BOOKS
by Dr. H. Edward Rowe
(Distributed by Growth Publishing)

THE ACLU AND AMERICA'S FREEDOMS	#071	2.95
by Ed Rowe		
HOMOSEXUAL POLITICS: ROAD TO RUIN FOR AMERICA	#070	2.95
by Ed Rowe		
THE DAY THEY PADLOCKED THE CHURCH	#005	3.50
by Ed Rowe		
NEW AGE GLOBALISM	#0143	5.95
by Ed Rowe		

BOOKS BY VARIOUS AUTHORS
(Distributed by Growth Publishing)

A CHRISTIAN MANIFESTO	#027	5.95
by Francis Schaeffer		
A TIME FOR ANGER	#026	6.95
by Francis Schaeffer		
BACKWARD MASKING UNMASKED	#006	4.95
by Jacob Aranza		

BAD NEWS FOR MODERN MAN	#049	7.95
by Franky Schaeffer		
BOOK BURNING	#017	5.95
by Cal Thomas		
CHANGE AGENTS IN THE SCHOOLS "A MUST"	#055	9.95
by Barbara Morris		
FOR THE CHILDREN'S SAKE	#089	6.95
by Susan Schaeffer Macualey		
GOD & CAESAR	#0115	7.95
by John Eidsmoe		
GOD'S TIMETABLE FOR THE 1980'S	#0104	5.95
by Dr. David Webber		
HOME EDUCATION & CONSTITUTIONAL LIBERTIES	#0114	5.95
by John W. Whitehead		
HOW SHOULD WE THEN LIVE (ILLUSTRATED)	#022	8.95
by Francis Schaeffer		
SCOPES II: THE GREAT DEBATE	#001	4.95
by Bill Keith		
THE ABORTION HOLOCAUST	#010	6.95
by Dr. William Brennan		
THE COMPLETE WORKS OF FRANCIS SCHAEFFER	#015	89.95
by Francis Schaeffer		
(5 Volumes Cloth)		

THE FREEDOM OF RELIGIOUS EXPRESSION IN THE PUBLIC SCHOOLS	#012	3.95
by John W. Whitehead		
THE GREAT EVANGELICAL DISASTER	#048	7.95
by Francis Schaeffer		
THE HIDDEN DANGERS OF THE RAINBOW	#007	5.95
by Constance Cumbey		
THE SEARCH FOR CHRISTIAN AMERICA	#019	6.95
by Noll/Hatch/Marsden		
THE STEALING OF AMERICA	#011	6.95
by John W. Whitehead		
TO HARASS OUR PEOPLE	#0100	6.95
by George Hansen		
TUITION TAX CREDITS	#056	5.95
by Barbara Morris		
VITAL SIGNS (A CHRISTIAN RESPONSE TO MEGATRENDS)	#0102	6.95
by Barna/McKay		
WHATEVER HAPPENED TO THE HUMAN RACE	#021	5.95
by Koop/Schaeffer		
WHY ARE YOU LOSING YOUR CHILDREN	#057	3.95
by Barbara Morris		

WHY J. R.? #003 4.95
  by Dr. Lew Ryder
WHO IS FOR LIFE #093 2.95
  by Mother Teresa/Schaeffer/Stott

TAPES THAT ARE
ABSOLUTELY MUST LISTENING

**BACKWARD MASKING
  UNMASKED** #098-Cas 5.95
  by Jacob Aranza
**THE HIDDEN DANGERS OF
  THE RAINBOW** #007-ALB 13.50
  (2 Tape Album)
  by Constance Cumbey
**THE STORY OF AMERICA'S
FIRST PADLOCKED
  CHURCH** #050-Cas 5.95
  by Dr. Everett Sileven

**WHO HAS THE CHILDREN
AND WHERE ARE THEY
TAKING THEM?** #068-ALB 39.95
  by Bill & Penny Bowen (an 8
  Tape Album Series)

Tape 1 EDUCATING FOR #060-Cas 5.95
  GLOBAL 2000

Lets Get A Handle
on Education!

Tape 2 GLOBALISM &		
GLOBAL EDUCATION	#061-Cas	5.95
Who's Who & What's What?		
Tape 3 ZERO POPULATION	#062-Cas	5.95
We've Got A Big Problem		
Tape 4 GLOBAL 2000 PART 1	#063-Cas	5.95
The Humanist Connection		
Tape 5 GLOBAL 2000 PART 2	#064-Cas	5.95
Deceit Aimed At The Christians		
Tape 6 A TANGLED WEB	#065-Cas	5.95
How Does It Affect Me?		
Tape 7 A NATION AT RISK	#066-Cas	5.95
The Demise Of America		
As We Know It.		
Tape 8 WHAT CAN I DO?		
***WE HAVE THE ANSWERS!**	#067-Cas	5.95
Parents In Alliance For		
Academic Education		

ESSENTIAL READING BY THE AUTHOR
OF THE ABOVE TAPE SERIES

GLOBALISM: AMERICA'S		
DEMISE	#0144	6.95
by William M. Bowen., Jr. Tpb		
GLOBALISM: AMERICA'S		
DEMISE (cloth)	#097	8.95

ORDER FORM

QTY.	ITEM NO.	DESCRIPTION	PRICE EACH	TOTAL EACH

METHOD OF PAYMENT

☐ Money Order　☐ Master Card　☐ Visa　☐ Check

Credit card No. ☐☐☐☐☐☐☐☐☐☐☐☐☐☐☐☐

Expiration date ☐☐☐☐☐

Telephone No. ( ) _____

Signature _____

TOTAL AMT.
ENCLOSED
(*in U.S. dollars*)
ADD 5% FOR SHIPPING

NAME _____

ADDRESS _____

CITY _____ STATE _____ ZIP _____

SEND ORDER TO:

GROWTH PUBLISHING
P.O. BOX 661
HERNDON, VIRGINIA 22070
OR CALL » 1 (800) 426-8095
In Virginia (703) 450-6460 or
1 (800) 533-4037

DISCOUNT SCHEDULE
1 THRU 10 NONE
11 THUR 24 20%
25 THUR 74 30%
75 PLUS 40%

INDEX